A Year in the Life...

52 Weeks of Quilting

Stories by Popser

Open Chain Publishing
Menlo Park, CA

Also by Popser in *A Year in the Life* series:
12 Months of Sewing

Cover and illustrations by Chris Hansen
Editing by Elin Thomas and Robbie Fanning
Proofreading by Mora Dewey

Copyright 2000 A.B. Silver

ISBN 0-932086-35-7

Printed in the United States of America

First printed November 2000
(Some stories have been reprinted in the *Creative Machine Newsletter, Quilt Magazine*, and England's *Popular Patchwork*.)

10 9 8 7 6 5 4 3

Note: The following are trademarked products: Kleenex, Kwik Klip, Kwik•Sew, Olfa, Post-it Notes, Stack-n-Whack, Velcro, Wonder-Under

Open Chain Publishing
PO Box 2634
Menlo Park, CA 94026-2634

(650)366-4440 • fax (650)366-4455
www.thecreativemachine.com
info@thecreativemachine.com

Foreword

Several years ago a man with the pen name of Popser began to write about his wife's love of sewing. He posted his stories on the Internet, where they were quickly disseminated around the world.

Then his wife discovered quilting, the fierce love of which only another enthusiast understands. Suddenly, a house becomes a quilting studio with a kitchen attached. Travels revolve around locations of fabric stores. Dreams are fabric-, thread-, and batting-filled. Popser had plenty of (apt word) material to draw on for stories.

Yet anyone who has lived for years with another person knows the possibilities for unintended humor, confusion, mutual exasperation, and joy. My favorite line in this entire book is "Are you in the same conversation I am?"

Popser *is* in conversation with Momser, and in the best way. He writes with affection and gentleness underlying his amusement with her antics. In doing so, he sparks memories in all of us about our own quilting adventures and our own mates.

Best of all, Momser keeps quilting and Popser keeps writing. You can read his latest stories at http://popser.com. I, for one, hope he'll write about what the quilting mates talk about while they wait for us outside the stores.

Robbie Fanning
Editor/Publisher, Creative Machine Newsletter
Co-author, The Complete Book of Machine Quilting

Contents

Introduction

*G*oing to the moon, exploring the inside of a volcano, traveling to Mars—few experiences match up to watching an otherwise sane woman take up quilting and disappear into a new universe, where nothing would ever be the same for either of us down here on earth.

I began these stories to sing out our joy at what great fun it was and ever is, to commiserate when necessary, and to share her quilting adventures with all those others who have had the same experiences.

I have been priviliged to travel alongside her and share her pursuit of the perfect quilt, from the first bewilderment and confusion to the first successes. The following stories reflect what I saw and heard during a year of her quilting life. And, of course, it goes on. How could I stop it? I invite you now to share in the experiences of my quilting wife in her quilting life.

A.B. Silver
Bakersfield, CA

Note: My thanks to Robbie Fanning, who sent the gift of her wonderful book on quilting to my Darling Wife and charmed her life by turning her into a quilter. I, of course, had to go along and, in order to survive, learn to understand the ups and downs and sideways of the beginning quilter's world.

And my eternal thanks, of course, to my Darling Wife, Joan, who in learning to take fabric, cut it apart, and sew it back together again, inspired these stories. She did all the real work. All I had to do was write down what happened. She still claims that I stretched the truth here and there, but, really, all I did was take her experiences and a few words and make a few crazy quilts of my own.

—ABS

PART 1

1. Fat What?

*W*hen in the course of human events the mailman brings a package that contains a book that changes history, it is best not to argue against God's will being done.

"What's in the package?" she asked. She had expected a copy of the *Creative Machine,* edited and published by Robbie Fanning. I took the newsletter from the package, but it was not alone. Attached to it with a large rubber band was a book.

"The *Creative Machine,*" I answered. "And some book."

"What kind of book?"

"I don't know," I said.

"Let me have it," my Darling Wife said. I gave her the book. She looked at it. I looked at her. She looked at me.

"It's a book about quilting," she said. "Why did you order a book about quilting? I don't quilt," she said.

"I know you don't quilt. I didn't order the book."

"Maybe it's for you?" she said. "Do you plan to quilt?" she asked. She wasn't serious. She couldn't be serious, could she?

"I don't plan to quilt," I said. "I never even plan to sew again. Never!" She knew all this.

I was her husband, her soul mate. I would support her in her sewing forever. But her sewing room was her life, and though I was her life mate, I had long before gone cold turkey and given up what little sewing I did to keep my buttons on. Now I don't even like using dental floss because it looks like thick thread and I'm afraid I'll sew my teeth together.

"There's a note attached," she said. "The book's a gift for me from Robbie." She showed me the note. She showed me the book: *The Complete Book of Machine Quilting*.

"Well, that explains it," I said wisely.

"It's a nice book," she said, "but I don't quilt."

"Well, maybe you could look at it some time."

"I don't have time to look at a book I'll never use. I have the Raggedy Ann doll to finish and then I have to make the two dresses for the girls." The girls are Shira and Rachel, two of our five grandchildren.

"Well, at least send a thank-you note."

"Why do you keep saying 'Well' all the time?" she asked.

"Well, why not?"

"Well, it's a nice book," she said. I looked at her in amazement. Her fingers were busy flipping the pages of the book. I watched as her head bobbed and her eyes turned down toward the colorful pages. "But I don't have time to look at it," she said, and she handed it to me.

"I'll put it away," I said as I reached for the book. But she pulled it back.

"It's a very nice book. Maybe I'll look at it, just for a minute."

And, well, that's the way it began. That was three weeks ago. Today I considered taking out a second mortgage on our house. Today I considered buying stock in every quilting store in the county. Today I asked her when she was going to sew again.

"Quilting is sewing," she said.

Three weeks and two hours after she received the book in the mail, she had looked through it all. Three weeks and four hours after, she received the book we were at the first quilting shop. Three weeks and six hours after, we were at a second quilting shop. Three weeks and eight hours after, late that same day, she owned an Olfa cutting mat and her first rotary cutter.

"What's a fat quarter?" she asked me that night.

"Fat what?" I asked.

"Fat quarter," she repeated.

I looked in my pocket and pulled out a quarter. I held it sideways. "Quarters aren't too fat," I said.

When I recovered from the blow to my stomach, I went to the computer and to the Internet. I typed in "Quilt," and the computer, like some angelic Las Vegas slot machine, spewed forth more information about quilting than I ever really wanted to see. Darling Wife was delighted. Did I just say delighted? She was euphoric, her smile spread across the room, the house, all of California.

"Print it all out," she said.

"There's not enough paper in the world to print it all out," I said.

"Print it out," she repeated. So I printed out a dictionary of quilting terms and a dozen helpful hints for beginners. (I suspect she became a beginner quilter when the mailman left the post office that fateful day.)

Tomorrow she starts her first class in quilting. She needs the class—for discipline. I tried to tell her about our limited budget, but her sense of reality disappeared the day the quilting kit for her sewing machine came in the mail. Her contact with reality faded when she watched the first of five quilting tapes she ordered (and that was before she discovered "Simply Quilts" and "Quilt in a Day" on television).

Perhaps the class will make her aware that she doesn't need a room full of fat quarters and a box full of templates and thirty spools of quilting thread and twenty yards of assorted fabric and every size plastic ruler and straight edge and quilting pins and needles and rolls of batting and open-toed walking and free-motion feet for her sewing machine. Perhaps, but I don't count on it.

The piles of squares and strips she has perfectly cut and sorted by complementary color schemes fill the cabinet where we used to keep cereal and flour. The crooked, misshapen, odd pieces of fabric which resulted from her first attempts with the rotary cutter are being saved for, as she puts it, "When I make a crazy quilt."

"You don't think you're going crazy about all this quilting?" I asked as I carried in the dozen different quilting magazines she sent me out to buy this morning.

"It's just sewing," she said. "And there's nothing crazy about sewing," she added as she took the magazines out of my hand.

"Of course not," I said. Of course not. How silly of me. Indeed!

2. Quilt Show

Husbands are free," she said.

"I haven't been free since I married you," I said.

"You'll save four dollars," she said.

"What will you buy with the four dollars I save?" I asked.

"I don't plan to buy anything. I just plan to look."

"I've heard that tune before," I said.

"I'm just going to look at the quilts. There's no charge for the husbands of quilters."

"That could be sexism," I said. "What if the husband is the quilter? Does the wife get in free?"

"You could ask when we get there," she said.

"So that means I'm going to the quilt show with you."

"You bet."

And so, not knowing whether I really wanted to see a lot of home made blankets, I went along to the show put on by the Cotton Patch

Quilters. I stood at the entrance while she paid her admission fee. I was getting in free. I peeked into the large hall to see what I would get for free. I saw lots of quilts. I saw about sixty million quilts. I turned to run, but she caught me and brought me back. "You'll live through it," she said, holding me tightly, wiping the sweat off my brow, and comforting me. "You'll be just fine," she said as she led me in.

"There are too many quilts," I said as I caught my breath and was able to talk again.

"That's why we're here, to see the quilts," she explained.

"Do I have to see them all?"

"Every one," she said.

"All right, but I won't look at all the stitches," I said, hoping to prevent her from asking me to examine each quilt as I knew she would.

And examine them she did. At the first quilt, something covered with big white spots, she peered at every square, every strip, every block, every stitch. She put on the white glove she was given at the entrance (I got in free so I didn't get a glove), and she turned the corner of the quilt to look at the backing. I looked at the small sign on the wall by the quilt. The quilt was called "Snowball Quilt." I didn't see any snow or feel cold. I didn't see a snowball or a snowman. All I saw was a very big design with a lot of white spots.

"I'll never be able to do this," my Darling Wife said as she lifted herself up from where she had bent down to see the bottom of the quilt.

"What are you doing on the floor?" I asked politely. She would have an answer.

"I'm looking at the binding," she said. She wiped dust off her knees.

"Couldn't you look at the binding on the sides?"

"I have to see it all," she said.

"Are you going to take this much time at every quilt?" I asked. We had been at the quilt for ten minutes.

"I'm learning how to quilt," she said. "I need to look at every one."

"Do I have to look at every one?"

She didn't answer me. She moved to the next quilt. "This is a Log Cabin quilt," she said.

"I don't see any cabins." I looked carefully, too. No log cabins, no houses built of straw or bricks either.

"I should have left you home," she said.

"I'm just taking an interest in your hobby," I said. It wasn't going to be a hobby. If she made a quilt, it would become her life. Sewing clothes for the newborn grandchildren had become her life. Sewing clothes when the infants became toddlers had become her life. Sewing clothes when they reached school age had become her life.

"This one's machine-quilted," she said.

"I thought quilts were made by eighty women sitting around a table with a needle and thread when they were snowed in all winter."

"This is a beautiful quilt," was all she replied, which told me to keep my mouth closed or she would stuff the whole quilt in it.

The next quilt was beautiful. The design, the pattern, the colors, the workmanship overwhelmed even this curmudgeon.

"I'm quitting," she said.

"You want to leave? After only three quilts?" I couldn't believe her. What had I said to upset her?

"I'll never be able to do this," she said, her voice shaky.

"In time," I said, trying to encourage her. "You're just starting out."

"I don't have time. I have all that other sewing."

"So it won't take you a day to make a quilt. You can spend the whole weekend on it. Later you'll get better and faster."

"This quilt took more than a weekend."

"Well, it is beautiful. So you'll take a week off your other sewing to finish a quilt."

She didn't reply. She pointed to the sign that identified the quilt. "This quilt took fourteen years to make," she said.

"Hah, you're kidding!" That look again. "You're not kidding? Fourteen years? A quilt took fourteen years? You're going to spend fourteen years on a quilt?" I could see her locked up in her room for fourteen years. I could see myself bringing her food and water and more fabric, more thread, replacement rotary cutter blades, truckloads of batting.

"I'm not going to spend fourteen years," she said with a sigh. "Besides, this is all hand quilted. I'm going to use my machine."

"So how long will it take when you use your machine?" How gray would my hair be by then? Would I have any hair left when she was finished?

"Well, I did see that video, 'Quilt in a Day.'"

"A day? A day's good."

"This is a beautiful quilt, all right," she said as she turned away from the masterpiece. "We shouldn't spend so much time on one quilt. Let's go look at the other quilts."

"We can just look at the day quilts," I said. "They'll be just the right size for day beds," I said, hoping like mad.

"We'll look at them all," she said. "Every stitch."

And we did. Oh, yes, we did. And yesterday she began her first class. Something about quilting with snowballs. Sounds cold to me.

3. Scraps

Help," I heard. The muffled sound came from the back of the house. I put down my book, waited a moment until I heard a second cry, "Helffflllgggg," then moved down the hallway to her sewing room. The door was closed, and when I tried to open it, it opened very slowly. I pushed harder and opened a wedge large enough for me to see into the room.

"Hon," I called into the room. My own sound was muffled, dampened by the piles of fabric hiding the floor. "You in here?" I asked as my eyes took in the piles of fabric covering the sewing machine, the serger, the chair. A cyclone had come into the room and deposited the contents of every trash can from every fabric store in the city.

"Mmmmphhhhh," I heard from the corner of the room, the sound squeezing out from a pile of multicolored scraps, a flower garden of scraps. I realized the whole room was inundated with scraps. I realized that somewhere in that madness of a gigantic fabric storm, my Darling Wife was calling for help.

I plowed through fabric squares, triangles, strips, cut and torn pieces of every size and shape. Behind me as I moved, a wake of scraps rippled toward the walls. I steeled myself, took a deep breath, and reached through mounds of trimmings and clippings toward the moving hump of fabric. I found my Darling Wife and pulled her up into daylight.

She choked and sputtered and coughed and hacked her mouth clear of lint and thread. "You all right?" I asked. I didn't ask her what happened. I didn't ask her what she had been doing buried in an avalanche of fabric detritus. I already knew.

I knew when three days before she had watched a video she had rented on how to make a scrap quilt. I knew during the three days I watched her search every room of the house, every box in the garage, every shelf and every drawer to gather her hidden stash of scraps. She had been saving her scraps for two years. "I might need them some day," she had told me for two years as she squirreled away the "leavings" of her sewing in every spare inch of space. For three days she had been "moving" the scraps into her sewing room.

"I'm fine. A few of the scraps fell off the shelf," she said calmly.

I brushed her off. "About a hundred pounds of scraps," I said.

"I forgot how much I had," she said. She was breathing normally again.

I brushed some small diamonds of paisley fabric out of her hair. "You have a lot," I said. "How big a quilt are you planning to make?"

"I'm not making a quilt yet. I've only had one lesson so far."

"But?"

"But I thought I could practice making a small scrap square. I don't have to worry too much about getting it perfect."

"Are you going to sew some of these scraps together, is that it?" I asked. She nodded. "How large a square?"

"Six inches," she said meekly.

"So you needed thirty truckloads of scraps to make a six-inch square."

"I need lots of practice. Besides, it's hard deciding which scraps to use."

"Why don't you close your eyes and reach down and grab a handful and use them?" That's a logical question, right?

"Oh, no. The scraps have to match."

"They have to match?" I was genuinely puzzled. "Isn't it called a scrap quilt because you use scraps?"

"They still have to match. They have to be the right colors, the right designs, the right shapes. A quilter can't just sew any two pieces of fabric together." She was indignant now.

"So quilters need to have enough fabric in their sewing rooms to outfit an army before they can make a six-inch square?"

"Experienced quilters don't. I'm a beginner. Experienced quilters just blink at the fabric and they have all the colors, all the tones, all the pieces coordinated perfectly. I can't do that yet. I'm just a beginner. It will take me a while to learn how. Now let me get to work." She kicked at the fabric on the floor and opened a path so she could move around.

"You won't go under again?" I asked.

"Not unless I'm looking for a special scrap."

"And then you'll be careful?"

"I'll try to be careful," she said.

"All right, then," I said as I turned to make my own path out of the room. It was a very colorful room, I admit.

"But a beginning quilter can't promise to be perfect," she added. She picked up a handful of scraps and examined them. I was dismissed.

I went back to the living room and began to read my book, but I couldn't concentrate. I kept hearing scraps falling. I know I did.

4. Unchained Melody

J thought I had gone back forty years, when wash hung from the line in the back yard, each garment waving in the gentle breeze. I remembered ducking under the flags of wash as they lifted and dropped in the wind. It was a colorful sight, one that years later the dryer eliminated from my life. But no longer. Her sewing room hung with ribbons of wash, and as I ducked under the tiny flags, I wondered where I was in time.

"Careful," she said as I grazed the color-draped line. She had looked up as I came in, but now she was back at the sewing machine, the machine humming along, a string of wash unloading itself from the back of the sewing machine.

"Are you drying clothes?" I asked. She stopped the machine in the needle-down position, probably to protect whatever new world she was sewing.

"Chain piecing," she said. "I learned it in class. Some people call it chaining or assembly-line piecing." She's always giving me little quilting lectures.

"It looks like a clothes line," I said.

"They're all patches pieced together. It saves time and tons of thread."

"How much time?" I had to ask her that first. Then I would ask her the serious questions.

"Hours. Days. Maybe months. I don't know yet. I'm a beginner." She ran her hand under the long strip of fabric that had come out of her machine. "They're all sewn together without cutting each one separately as I sew," she explained. "That's the slow way."

"Oh," I said, as if I understood. I shook my head and turned to look across the lines of wash. Sure enough, they were all tiny squares stitched to each other. What at first appeared to be little dresses or pants or underwear or cotton robes were really several two-and-a-half-inch square patches sewn together, one group after another after another. "It doesn't look like a quilt," I said.

"Not yet," she said.

"But it will be?"

"It'll be squares. Lots and lots of squares."

"They look like tiny clothes," I said.

"They're not little clothes," she said impatiently. "I have to snip them and sew them together yet."

"How many times?"

"About a thousand, I think. Maybe more."

"And then you'll have a quilt?"

"No, then I'll have twenty-five big squares, each made up of nine little squares."

"Then what?"

"Then I have lesson two. I haven't gotten there yet."

"But you will?"

"Next week."

"How do you know which direction to sew them together?" I asked.

"That's the hard part."

"Knowing east and west and south and north?"

"Knowing clockwise or counter-clockwise, front side and back side."

I didn't comment on that last part.

"Why did you pick these colors?"

"They go together," she said.

"They're very nice the way they go together," I said, "but it really looks like a long clothesline with tiny little clothes." I wasn't about to give up. I tested my senses as I looked at them. I touched them. Then I saw the small chain of stitching joining them together. They were colorful pieces of fabric. But they looked like my old clothesline.

"You don't see any clothespins, do you?"

"They're probably too tiny to see."

"How about you becoming too tiny to see?" she said. She pressed her foot down on the foot pedal. The needle lifted up and down again. Fast. She stoked the machine with fabric and made more squares.

"Humph," I said as I turned to leave. "You're chained to that machine."

"Chain-piecing," she said. "And you belong on a chain gang."

"I think I'll go chain myself to dinner," I said, ducking my head as I left, wondering if the white meat of turkey went with the green of the peas and the brown of the gravy. And I wondered how the servings would look in squares. "I have a great idea for a quilt," I added, but she didn't seem to hear me. Not one last word.

PART 2

5. Rubik's Square

I always hated Rubik's Cube," she said. She was sitting on the floor next to her flannel board, arranging the nine-patch squares she had made for her quilt.

I accepted the invitation to have a conversation with her. "I didn't like it much either," I said. "My hands always hurt afterwards."

"My hands don't hurt," she said. She was staring at the forty-nine squares in front of her.

I tried another answer. "I didn't like Rubik's Cube because I never could do it."

"It drove me crazy," she said. Ah, now we were getting close to it.

"It drove me a little crazy, too," I said.

"My head doesn't do spatial relations," she said. "Nothing ever matched up. Not then, not now."

Oh, oh, this was heading somewhere. "What about not now?" I asked carefully, gently.

"Twelve squares are wrong," she said. "Twelve of them look just like a Rubik's cube."

"I don't see anything wrong," I said, as I looked where she was looking. The design for the Snowball quilt looked fine. Actually, I was dazzled by it and impressed by all the work my Darling Wife had done.

"I didn't see it before either," she said. "I started sewing the squares together and didn't even begin to see it." She moved to the flannel board then and started to move one of the squares. The nine patches in the square were made up of two patches each of four different calico fabrics with a white patch in the middle. She turned the square around and around and around. I got dizzy watching her.

"It looks fine any way you turn it," I said, trying to be helpful, trying to contribute to her quilting joy.

"It's wrong any way I turn it," she said. She went to another square and began rotating it. Then she switched that square with another square. She rotated both squares, one with each hand. My eyes were on a spinning pinwheel.

"What's wrong with it?" I asked. Someone had to ask that question. It was time for a reality check.

"It's backwards. It's upside-down. It's turned around. It's counter-clockwise instead of clockwise. It's clockwise instead of counter-clockwise."

"Well, that explains it," I said. Now I was not only dizzy but, in trying to keep up with her, my head had rotated one hundred eighty degrees.

"It won't work. I did some of the squares backwards or sideways."

"Well, you can take them apart and do it the way it should be." I always tried to encourage her.

"I can take you apart and put you back together the way you should be," she said. She pulled a square off the board and then another and then another.

"How many?" I asked when she was done and the quilt top looked as if she had used a shotgun on it.

"Twelve. I did twelve wrong." She held a pile of squares and stared at them. Then she tossed them aside with a sigh.

"Can't you take them apart and re-sew them?" What did I know?

"There are ten billion tiny stitches holding the patches together," she said. I took that as a negative answer.

"What are you going to do with them?" Maybe she could punish them in some way.

"I can use them for something else. I'll make a doll quilt or a wallhanging or a snore quilt."

"A snore quilt? What's a snore quilt?"

"Something to put over your face when you sleep to stop you from snoring." She smiled, and I knew she had forgotten Rubik's Cube.

"What about this quilt?"

"I'll make twelve new squares and do them right."

"And you'll make them perfect this time?"

"It's my first quilt. It won't be perfect."

"There, then," I said in a positive manner. What else could I have said?

"But it'll be almost perfect," she said. "Something like you. Almost perfect. After I finish the quilt, I'll start on you."

"No, you'll have another quilt to make," I suggested quickly. "Or a doll. Or a dress. Something."

"You'd better hope so," she said.

I'm hoping. She's in the other room now cutting strips for the new squares, and I'm really hoping.

6. Up to Batt

I'm going to have to learn about batting," she said.

"Baseball or quilting?" I asked.

"It's too early for baseball," she said.

"Then batting for your quilt?" I asked.

"Three kinds," she said.

"Three kinds of batting?"

"Four-ounce, six-ounce, and ten-ounce," she said.

"Thin and thick and thicker?"

"Yes. The quilt store has a sale today."

"And we're going to the sale?"

"Absolutely," she said.

And so we went out to buy some batting.

"What's the difference between batting and bunting?" I asked as we drove along toward the store.

"In baseball or quilting?"

"Quilting," I guess. I usually guess "quilting" as the answer to most questions she asks.

"Bunting's for babies," she said.

"Isn't bunting used for making flags?"

"Yes, that's the cloth used for making flags."

"What about the babies? Do they need flags?"

" A baby bunting is like a baby sleeping bag with a hood."

"And someone wrote a poem about it?"

"What?" she said.

"I remember a nursery rhyme. Something about bunting a baby, wasn't it?" She gave me that look and began reciting one of the ten million nursery rhymes she knew.

"Bye, baby bunting/Daddy's gone a'hunting/Mummy's gone a'milking/Sister's gone a'silking/Brother's gone to buy a skin/To wrap the baby bunting in," she said smugly.

"I should have known you'd know that," I said.

"It has nothing to do with batting," she said.

"They don't use baby flags for batting?" I asked. "Maybe they wrapped babies in the flags when the babies were cold or wet." Why not?

"Drive," she said.

I drove and we arrived at the shop and we went to the corner of the store where the batting was on sale. There were several bins with rolls of batting in each one. "Do you know why batting is called 'batting'?" I asked.

"You know why?"

"I'm a Quilting Spouse," I said. "I'm supposed to know that."

"All right," she said, humoring me. "Why is batting called 'batting'?"

"Well, it might even have been called 'beating,'" I said. "I'm not sure about that part."

"I'm waiting," she said as she reached into one of the bins. The roll of batting was taller than she was and three times wider.

"People used to beat raw cotton to clean it. Batt may have meant the stick, or bat, used to beat the cotton or wool to clean it," I said without batting an eye.

"Are you sure?" She struggled with the large roll of batting. I reached for it and took it out of the bin.

"I'm not sure of anything except this is a lot of batting. How much do you need?"

"Fifteen inches of each weight," she said. "But I'm going to get a yard of each."

"Just in case?" I asked. That was her reasoning for buying more of anything that she needed. If she needed one quilting pin, she would buy two hundred fifty. Just in case.

"You think I should get two yards," she answered.

"I think one yard will do you for this week," I said. She knew where the store was, the store hours, and where everything was.

I grabbed the roll of batting. Now all I had to do was carry it twenty yards to the cutting table. It was not heavy. It was bulky. I bumped my way across the twenty yards. I hit only two shelves, one display of quilting notions, and a row of bolts of fabric. Behind me the floor became littered. My Darling Wife was right behind me, picking up and replacing each item and restoring the swaying shelves back to normalcy.

"One yard," I said to the amused clerk who stood behind the cutting table.

"You could have bought it in the smaller package," she said helpfully.

"Is the smaller package on sale?" I asked.

"No."

"One yard," I said. I was broke enough for this day already.

When she cut the yard, I hefted the roll of batting and carefully wended my way back to the bins. This time Darling Wife guided me carefully through the maze of shelves and racks of fabric. I knocked down only one small display of rotary cutters. Then I put the roll of batting away and reached for the second roll.

Ten minutes later, having knocked only one woman dizzy as I turned a corner with the roll of ten-ounce batting, we had the batting rolled into plastic bags and we were on our way home.

"Do you know what you are going to do with this batting?" I asked.

"I'm going to use it when I take the machine-quilting class next month."

"Next month? And you have everything you need now?" I asked. If not now, when?

"I think so," she said, and she pulled out the two-page list of materials she needed for the class. She read it for a moment. "Uh-oh," she said.

"'Uh-oh' as in you forgot something?" I asked, "or 'uh-oh' you need some baby bunting?"

"I got the wrong batting," she said.

"Go on."

"I need three different *brands* of batting, so we can compare brands. Not three different weights." She was not apologetic, not concerned in the least. She would add the batting to her stash of "Someday." Somedays were hidden all over our house. If she didn't use them today, well, then, maybe someday.

"You want to go back now?" I asked as I drove into our driveway.

"Do you mind?"

"No, of course not. After all, next month will be here in thirty days."

7. Winner Takes All

Lately, my Darling Wife, Mother of our children, Blessed Grandmother, and Quilting Queen, had become a stranger. Oh, I knew who she was. I even knew where she was most of the time. But she had become so entangled in her sewing, her projects, that it was becoming more and more difficult to recognize her. Occasionally I could see some of her face, maybe an elbow or a knee, and yesterday when she went in to shower, I caught a blur of skin.

"I'm quilting," she would say to me when I wanted to stop her for a meal together, a few minutes in front of the TV, a moment before bed.

"I wouldn't have known that by looking at you," I would say. Not only were her clothes good signs of what she was doing, their original look lost to the bits and pieces of thread and fabric that clung all over her, but her hair, too, had lost its graceful gray to become a rainbow of bits and scraps of color, some of which even the owner of the most punk hairdo would envy.

"I look like any person who sews a little," she said, dismissing my attempts to find the original woman I once knew behind that lint and thread disguise.

And I thought she was unique. She had her own peculiar way of looking, and I accepted it along with her need to breathe, eat, drink, and sew. But when last Saturday she took me along to the fabric store to buy a yard of yellow cotton to use in the making of her quilt, I realized she had relatives. Not blood relatives in her family or relatives by marriage. No, she had an extended family that had ties everywhere. Some of them were at the fabric shop.

"So, what are you working on now?" I heard from a woman standing by the dozen bolts of yellow 100% cotton. Each bolt was a different shade of yellow, a different tone, a different degree of brightness. The small woman was up on her toes, stretching herself to reach the top shelf above the yellow bolts. I began to answer that I wasn't working on any projects except sloth, lethargy, and indolence, but she wasn't talking to me or my Darling Wife, who was getting her yellow fabric. She was talking to a taller woman who was helping bring down a bolt of tan fabric.

I looked at both women. One was wearing a blue-flowered print summer dress and the other had on a pink halter top and white shorts. At least that's what they wore underneath. Attached in some mysterious way to the tall woman's clothes was an array of colored threads and scattered bits of blue fabric. The shorter woman had red strands of thread woven among the auburn hair that curled above her happy face.

"I see by your outfit that you're sewing today," the shorter one said as she took the bolt of fabric and cradled it in her arms.

"I never have a chance to get all the thread off," came the answer. To prove her point, the taller one swiped at her clothes without effect.

"I never can get clean either," the shorter one said. "I don't try anymore."

"I know what you mean. Look at me." She made herself even taller as she pointed to a red thread on her shoulder. "That's from a blouse I was making last week."

"That's nothing," said the second. "This piece of batik came from a wallhanging I was quilting last month."

"Where'd you buy the fabric?" asked the tall woman as she touched the batik.

"Here," she said. "In the back of the shop."

"I got this here, too," she said as she pulled off a tiny green thread. "It's Sea Mist."

By this time two other woman and a man had gathered around. I was suddenly aware that I was out of place. My blue T-shirt was clean. My white shorts and white socks were clean. I didn't belong here. Not with these victims of "Sewer's Cling Syndrome." I didn't have a single piece of thread or fabric clinging to my clothes to prove I was sewing something in my life. I was an outsider.

I looked at the small group, all dusted with proof of their sewing, threads and small colored motes of lint, bits of fabric clinging to their lives.

"You've been doing a Churn Dash," said the man to one of the women. "I see the pieces you cut off," he said, approaching her to look more closely at microscopic strips of black and purple on her polka-dotted dress.

"Three weeks ago. I finished it and gave it as a wedding present." She fingered the decorative remnant across her waist proudly.

"This is from taking in a pair of slacks," the gentleman said pointing, with just a touch of humble pride in his voice, to a triangular piece of gabardine.

"I have this," a new woman said as she approached. The group widened to let her in. She was pointing to a flowered yo-yo the size of a dime. "It's from a vest I was making eight months ago," she said, but there was sadness in her voice. "I never finished. I got started on something else and never went back."

More people joined in. The voices seemed to get louder then, scream-ing all around me, each one louder than the next, all pointing and touching and explaining. I looked for my Darling Wife. I saw her just outside the circle of thread-covered humanity. I reached out for her, grabbed her hand, and pulled her into the circle. "Stop," I cried out to the assembled crowd. "Look at this." I turned her around for all to see.

"What is it?"

"I don't see anyone."

"A pile of remnants, that's all."

"Is there someone there?"

"Is this a joke?"

"Who?"

I took hold of the pile of color in front of me, the scraps, the thread, the lint, the dropped stitches, the corners, the ends, the torn selvages, and I shook the woman I love. I shook and I shook until an avalanche of sewing debris fell to the floor and uncovered my Darling Wife.

"Ooh."

"Ahhh."

"She certainly knows how to sew."

"She wins," I said as I pulled her, the bolt of yellow fabric, and myself toward the checkout counter.

It was a unanimous decision.

8. Squilt Guilt

I need a hand," she said. She stood next to me at the kitchen table as I took what was going to turn out to be my last sip of coffee for the morning.

"A hand or a whole body?" I asked. I knew her code. I knew she wouldn't be content with just a hand. But I didn't know she would want my whole body.

"Come on," she said in a tone that would tolerate no further questions. I was to be hers. Mine was not to reason why.

I managed to put my cup and empty breakfast plate onto the kitchen counter before she whisked me out of the kitchen and into the living room. "What? What is it?" I asked.

"I need to baste the quilt," she said.

"You have the top all finished?" I asked, surprised that it was done. The night before she still had the last border to sew on.

"I've been up since two," she said.

"And you finished the top?" I asked without purpose. Of course she had finished the top. "And you finished the back, too?" She nodded ever so slightly, and that was enough to know she had been one very busy bee.

"I need a hand in making the squilt," she said. She was ready to sandwich the top and the batting and the back.

"You want me to help you put it together?" I was bewildered. Perhaps she hadn't had enough sleep. If I touched the quilt she was making, it would fall apart. It would disintegrate before our eyes. I was as handy with a piece of fabric and a needle and thread as a hibernating bear, which is one animal I envied just then.

"Of course not," she said with that cute little dismissing laugh of hers. "I need room to spread the quilt out so I can baste it."

"In here?" I asked, bewildered as I looked around the living room, looked at the sectional, the fireplace, the table of plants by the window, the coffee table, the stereo system, the television, the clear lack of space for anything more.

"It's the only place in the house with enough room," she insisted.

"I can move the coffee table, I suppose," I said. If I moved the coffee table there might be just enough space to lay the squilt on the carpeted floor.

"I can't work on the floor," she said, putting a quick end to that idea.

"So?" I asked, which of course is the worst question in the world to ask when I would have been much better off just running out of the house, getting into the car, and driving three thousand miles to the East Coast, regardless of what the weather was.

"I want you to bring in the folding tables and set them up."

I laughed, but it was a very short laugh. "In here?"

"I need lots of room," she said. "You'll have to move something."

"I'll have to move something," I muttered to myself. "I'll have to move something," I said to her. I hoped she would appreciate my smile as I spoke. What I would have to move was the ten-ton sectional.

"I'll help," she said. Hah!

She helped all right. She steered me as I swung my body low ("sweet chariot"), put my back to one side of the couch ("tote that barge"), and grunted a while without budging the couch one bit ("that lucky old sun has nothing to do but roll around heaven all day").

She helped all right. She pointed at the hearth eight feet away and said, "Just push it over here."

I pushed. I shoved. I stood up and straightened out twenty-two kinks in my back. I pulled. I grunted. I stooped over. I pushed some more. The couch moved an inch, another inch, a third inch. "Is that enough?" I asked.

"Just a drop more," she said.

And so it went. Eight lives later, I had the sectional up against the hearth. I had moved the coffee table. I had taken the plants and the table they were on away from the window. I had cleared a space large enough for the overseer to work. I had depleted my body of any energy it might ever have again and had pulled every muscle in my body to a place where no muscle had gone before.

"Now you can bring in the tables and set them up," she said.

"Now?"

"I've been up since two," she said. That was answer enough. I went into the garage to get the two six-foot long banquet tables we used twice a year when we had enough courage to have our children, their spouses, and our grandchildren over for dinner all at one time.

Of course, when I was in the garage, I looked at the tables and seriously considered what life was like before she took up quilting.

Before, she only had two rooms devoted to her sewing. Now, it seemed, the living room had been added to her sewing estate.

So, I gave up on ever knowing my body again and maneuvered the two tables through the kitchen, through doorways that weren't designed for any easy passage, and into the living room, where they just happened to set up into one large "quilting table."

"Good job," my Darling Wife said. That gracious acknowledgment of my work was my only reward (except for the loss of six gallons of sweat and three pounds). But it was certainly reward enough.

"Now you have a place to work," I said.

"It's very nice," she said, but she said it in a very odd way.

"Oh?"

"Well," she said sweetly.

"Well, what?" I said, less sweetly.

"Well, while you were in the garage I called Sharon at the quilting shop and asked her advice and she offered me her tables. She has those four big tables, and I can spread everything out so much better and tape down the back, and she's there to help me, so I'm going to baste the quilt there. I'll be back soon," she said.

"You'll be back soon?" I asked. I had already lost my body. Was I about to lose my mind? "What about this room?"

"Oh, leave it the way it is. I'll need the tables when I start the machine quilting. I'll just move my sewing machine in here. You don't mind, do you?"

The quilt is basted now, and I am resting now. I think I'll just rest here a while longer. A while longer. A while longer. A while longer….

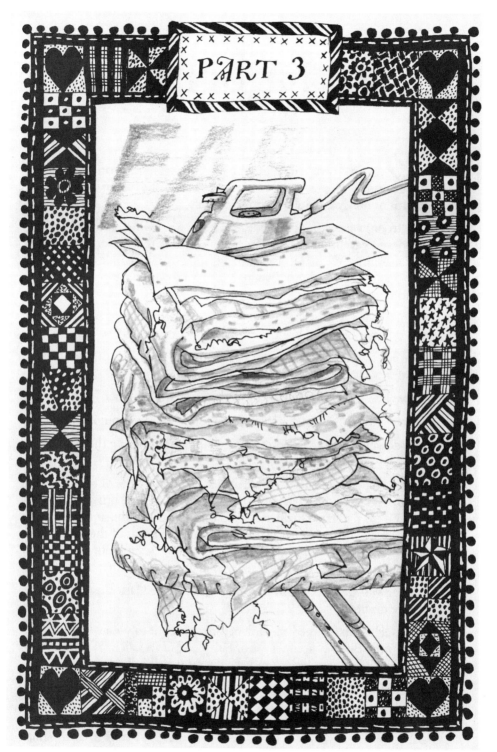

PART 3

9. Her Schedule

One-fifty-two," she said. She was clearing a space on the refrigerator door, pushing aside family photos. She had just pushed photos of our grandchildren off to the left.

I didn't answer her. I had no idea what she was saying, and any response I gave might get me into more trouble than I wanted late that morning. We had just returned from a trip forty miles away to visit two new quilt shops. I waited and worked on the sandwich I was creating for my lunch.

"What about two-twelve?" she asked. I smeared mustard on both slices of my 42-Grain bread.

"Sounds fine," I said. I put the sliced turkey over the mustard. I had no idea what she was asking this time either.

"If we find a good stencil, I can work on the quilt border."

"Sure," I said. I put in the lettuce and tomato and red onion.

"Or do you think I should read the chapter on mitering the binding?"

"Sounds good," I agreed. I looked away from the slices of bell pepper I had just cut to see what she was doing now. She had put a piece of paper onto the space she had cleared on the refrigerator, and she stood there with a red felt pen in her hand, the point of the pen inches away from the paper. On the paper were several notations, but from where I stood I couldn't see well enough to read them.

"Or do you think I should finish the doll I started last week? Maybe before dinner."

"I thought you finished the doll before you went to your quilting class at the Bobbin Spinner Wednesday." I put the slices of bread together, held them down, and cut the sandwich in half.

"No, I don't think so. What about the embroidery?"

"What?"

"I have to do my first embroidery. I've had the new sewing machine a week and I haven't tried out the embroidery attachment."

"So, why haven't you done any embroidery?"

"I was learning how to do the memory."

"What's the machine supposed to remember?"

"All the stitches," she said. She wrote something on the paper. "I'll have to do it tomorrow after we get back from Strawberry Patches."

"You're going shopping again?" I asked.

"We have to get some binding clips," she said.

"*We* have to get some binding clips?"

"Do you trust me to go alone? You remember what happened last time, don't you?"

I did remember her buying the twelve yards of muslin she would certainly need to have in the house in case every muslin manufacturer went out of business the next day. "What time?" I asked. She had already committed my Saturday morning to surf the Internet for quilting sites.

"Two-forty-six," she said.

"I have that time slot free," I said. I wondered why not two-forty-five or two-forty-seven. I carried the sandwich over to the refrigerator and looked at what she was writing down in bold red ink.

"Shopping list?" I asked.

"Schedule," she said.

"What kind of schedule?"

"Sewing schedule," she said. "I have a lot of things to sew."

"So you need a schedule?"

"I keep forgetting what I'm supposed to sew. Yesterday I forgot to shorten the sleeves on your shirt. This morning I was supposed to practice my free-motion quilting."

"We went to the new quilt shops this morning."

"See. I already forgot that. Where did I put the fabric I bought? I have to serge up the edges and wash it. I keep forgetting what I'm doing."

"Maybe you're doing too much," I suggested. Rather, I should have washed my mouth out with Plumber's Helper.

"There's never too much. I just have to remember it all."

"I thought you wrote down all your projects," I said, remembering her long list of sewing things to do.

"I have my list. I just don't know when I'm supposed to do everything."

"You don't know when to do the sewing and the quilting and the doll making and the embroidery?"

"That reminds me," she said without answering. "I need to buy some embroidery thread."

"*We,*" I reminded her, "are going to Strawberry Patches tomorrow."

"Are we?" she said. I nodded. I really wanted to sit down and eat my sandwich. "See, I forgot about that."

"You know what," I began, interrupting myself so at least I could smell the sandwich, "maybe you should make some kind of plan to do all the things you have to do."

"I'm trying to do that, but you keep interrupting me," she said as she pushed me aside. She made some more marks on her paper. "Can't you see I'm trying to make a schedule?"

"Am I going to be on your schedule?"

"You?" she looked at me. She looked at the schedule. She made a red splotch on her schedule, some kind of Rorschach Sewing Test for me, no doubt.

"Well?"

"How about eight-fifty-seven next Sunday night?"

10. Notice Anything?

Well, do you notice anything different?" she asked as I walked into the bedroom. Now, when she asks me that question I look at her very carefully. I looked at her hair, her clothes, her earrings, her shoes, her hands and feet and then back up to her head again. And the way she asked the question made me look very hard.

"No," I said.

"Look again," she said. I started to look again, but she quickly danced out of my sight. "Not me, Silly," she said in a teasing manner that made me rethink my looking strategy.

"You look fine, terrific, great," I said, just in case she might have done something to herself that I should have noticed.

"Look around. What do you see?" she hinted. At least it was something that could be seen.

"Is it bigger than a bread box?" I asked. "Smaller?"

"You had better notice," she said, her tone just a bit heavy with threat. Boy, did I look around. Fast and hard.

Everything looked the same. The bed. The dresser. The closet. The window. The chair. The bed! I looked back at the bed. "You made the bed," I said, my voice heavy with a friendly smile. It was not the right thing to say.

"What's on the bed?" she asked coolly.

"The sheets, the blanket, the bedspread, the quilt."

"What was that last thing you said?" she asked.

I looked at the bed again. "The quilt," I said.

"And just what quilt is that?" she asked.

And then the dawn, the electric light bulb, Archimedes' cry of "Eureka!"

"You finished the quilt," I said.

"I'm about to finish you," she said.

"It looks great. It's marvelous! Wonderful! Beautiful! Magnificent! A masterpiece!"

"So, what do you really think?" she asked.

"I really think you finished your quilt." I went over to the bed and looked down at the finished quilt. All the patches, all the squares, all the borders, all the binding, all the quilted stitches were there. It was lovely.

"And do you like it?"

"What's not to like?" I asked.

"You really like it?"

"It's perfect."

"It's not perfect. Just don't look too close. It's just my first quilt."

"Do you like it?" I asked.

"A little."

"Just a little?"

"A lot."

"Just a lot?" She was very modest.

"A whole lot," she said. She was aglow now.

"Do you want to celebrate?" I asked.

"I already celebrated," she said.

"How? How did you already celebrate without me?"

"I shouted. I yelled. I laughed out loud."

"Is that all?"

"That was enough. I did celebrate every day I worked on it, you know."

"You did?"

"Every night I celebrated that I hadn't ruined it that day."

"I celebrated, too, you know." I lifted the quilt and held it up and it was some fine quilt.

"What did you celebrate?" she asked.

"Every night I celebrated that you were making a quilt."

"But it wasn't finished then. How did you know I would finish it? I wasn't that sure myself."

"Quilting husbands know things like that."

"I didn't know you were a quilting husband. I thought you were just a tolerant husband with an incredibly insane wife."

"Quilting husbands are insane, too. It's just a quieter, more gentle kind of insanity."

"All right," she said, accepting whatever I had just admitted to. I wasn't sure what that was. "Where do you think I should hang it?" she added, turning the moment around.

"Hang it?" I asked.

"The quilt. I have to hang it. It's my first quilt. You said you like it, didn't you?"

"I love it, and we can hang it on one of those poles in the front of the house. We can put up a pole that will make all those other funny nylon flags people fly in front of their houses look like pieces of belly-button lint next to your quilt."

"Quilts don't hang outside. Besides, I'm not a show-off."

"Remember when we were in Pennsylvania and we saw all those quilts hanging outside people's houses. Some were just hanging over the fences along the road."

"They were for sale," she said.

"Then we can sell yours and…." Oops! I think I ate the rest of my words.

"This is *not* for sale," she said very loudly.

"You would never want to sell your first quilt," I agreed. "Absolutely not."

"But I can make another quilt."

"Yes, you can."

"And another and another and another and another and…."

Today she started on a new quilt. When it's finished, it will be her second quilt. And I plan to notice it the moment it's finished. And we will celebrate together. I promise.

11. Strike While the Iron's Hot

Help!" she called out from the garage. She seemed in great and immediate pain, so I finished lunch, rinsed the dishes, put away the paper I had been reading, checked the messages on the telephone, then rushed to her aid. I found her with her arms deep into the washing machine bringing out a load of "wash." Her pain was merely a lot of grunting as she lifted the load.

"I can't go on like this. I want to quilt," she said, muffling her voice with the damp laundry.

"You want me to help carry that?" I asked kindly as she dumped the large mountain of rags against me to take. I took the load. It was ninety-four degrees out that day and hotter in the garage. The damp laundry felt good.

She bent back inside the deep cavern of the washing machine for a few stray pieces, which she piled on top of what she had already given me. "Take that to the ironing room," she said.

"Ironing room?" I asked in panic. Did we now have an ironing room hidden somewhere in the house? My office was the last free space in the house not already taken up with her quilting empire. Had she taken over that room, too, in her quest for more territory?

"The sewing room," she said in answer to my desperate question.

"You need to do some more ironing?" I talked into cotton.

"Go," she said. I went as she guided me into the house, through the kitchen, down the hall to her sewing room. Finally, I was able to dump the load onto her sewing table, but she guided the laundry and me over to a plastic bag she had spread out on the floor next to the ironing board.

"What are you going to quilt?" I asked as I caught my breath.

"I'm not quilting anything," she said. "I may never quilt again." She picked at the pile of wash.

"May I ask why not?" I asked.

"I have to iron," she said.

"Oh," I said in my most comforting manner.

She glared at me. "All I ever do is iron," she said.

"I'm not that dirty," I said, looking now for the first time into the pile of "wash" to see how much of my clothing had added to her work. All I found were pieces of colored fabric. Large pieces of fabric. Smaller pieces of fabric. Tiny pieces of fabric. Blue, black, green, yellow, red, brown. Lots of black. None of my clothes was in the pile. "It's all your fabric," I said.

"I know. It's some of the fabric we bought yesterday," she said.

"You washed it and now you have to iron it," I said. It was not a question. She always washed her new fabric before she sewed anything. It was "rule twelve," she had long before told me. Or maybe "rule twenty." Quilting had a lot of rules.

"I have to iron it and fold it and put it away so I can be ready to quilt," she said.

"So, what's the big problem?"

"That's only the fabric I bought yesterday."

"Yes, I know," I said, remembering the long drive to the fabric shop, the long drive home, the long drive back after I discovered I had left my credit card at the shop, the second pile of fabric she bought because we were already there anyway and "why waste the trip?", and the long drive home again with six more yards of black cotton fabric for the Amish quilt she planned to make "later in the summer."

"UPS came this morning," she said simply. She turned on the iron and put it on the ironing board.

"And?"

"The twelve yards of white-on-white muslin came today. I still have to wash and iron that."

"So, you have a lot of ironing to do?"

"More ironing to do than all the laundries in the city."

"You didn't have to buy so much fabric," I said. It was a reasonable thought. "No fabric, no washing, no ironing." It was also a very dumb thing to say to woman who has found that life without fabric is a life without sustenance.

"I have to have the fabric for the quilt I'm going to make you." She paused and I was going to tell her she had enough fabric for a hundred quilts, but she wasn't finished. "And all the projects I have to do that I haven't thought up yet."

"And they'll all require pre-washing and pre-ironing and pre-folding?"

"Lots of ironing," she moaned.

"So, when will you be finished?"

She looked down at the pile of fabric in thought. "Next year," she said confidently.

"That soon?"

"Maybe later."

"You bought all this fabric, which will support three or four fabric mills, you know, just so you can use it all up quilting and then have to buy more?"

"Quilting's what I do now," she said.

"And ironing," I said. "Lots and lots of washing and ironing."

"I could iron you," she said.

"I'm leaving," I said.

"You have to come back for the folding," she said.

"The folding?"

"You're in charge of folding."

"I am?" Of course I was. And since she took up quilting, I've gotten very good at it.

"You don't mind?" she asked as she lifted her iron.

"Folding's what I do," I said. "Folding's what life is all about."

12. Stop and Shop

It would have been simple if we had just gone to the mountains and relaxed and walked and did a little hiking as we had planned. But the day after we arrived in Mammoth Lakes in northeastern California, she told me about the shop we had passed twenty-four hours and forty miles back.

"It's down in Bishop," she said.

"What's down in Bishop?" I asked. We had stopped in the small town for gas, but aside from a decent price for gas, I didn't remember much more than that we were there.

"I saw a window there with writing on it."

"Writing? What kind of writing?"

"Well, it was really printing."

"Printing? What kind of printing?"

"I'm not sure. I saw an F and an A and maybe a B."

"FAB?"

"You were driving too fast to see it all. It was a little blurry."

"There was more?"

"I think it was F-A-B-R-I-C," she said. We couldn't have been going more than twenty-five miles an hour at that time, but even if I had been going a hundred, she would not have missed a sign about sewing or fabric or quilts even if the letters had been only an inch high.

"Fabric?"

"I think so."

"But you're not sure?"

"I'm almost certain."

"And, I suppose, you want to drive back forty miles to see if the blurry letters you saw were part of a sign on a fabric shop?"

"You got it, Babe."

So, of course, after lunch we drove back down the mountain to the town of Bishop and, sure enough, there was a shop there that had a large sign on it that read *FABRIC.* And underneath was the shop's name: Sew It Seams.

"That was really a nice shop," she said afterwards as she put the bag of quilting books and stash into the car.

"That was a nice shop," I agreed, "and you spent all our gas money for the week. I guess we'll have to stay here forever."

"Don't be silly," she said. "Besides, there's another place to stop."

"There is?"

"The Fabric Store," she said. "I saw it as we were coming into town before. I don't know how I missed it yesterday." I didn't know how she missed it either. Somehow, she never misses.

"Didn't you go to a fabric store with a similar name when we stopped last month in Memphis?" I remembered because I just recently made out a check to pay the bill. I wondered how many fabric shops with the same name existed.

"That was a shop, not a store," she answered without hesitation. "The Fabric Shop," she said.

"You remember the exact name of the shop in Memphis?" Of course she would. If the name had the word fabric in it, she would remember it. If the name hinted at fabrics or sewing or quilting, she would remember it.

"Of course," she said. "Now drive."

I drove. An hour later, having stopped again at the second shop, and having spent our gas money for the year, we were on our way back up the mountain, only a half mile from where we were staying, when she saw another sign.

"Fabrications," she said. I looked. Among a strip of small shops about a block away, she had seen the sign.

"Good eyes," I said. I didn't want to think about another fabric shop. I really wanted to get up to the lakes and walk around and breathe the clean high-mountain air. Though it was middle June, some of the lakes were frozen over and much snow still covered the mountains. I wanted to walk in the snow.

"Stop there," she said, and she pointed into the parking lot in front of what turned out to be another fabric shop. No doubt Noah had two fabric shops aboard the Ark just waiting to reproduce. And reproduce they did.

I stopped and we went in and she shopped.

We are home now, home in a town where we have two quilt shops and three fabric shops, but is she satisfied? No. She wants to see every fabric and quilt shop in the country. How many of them are there? I don't want to know. I don't want her to know. The adventure for her is to sniff them out, to traipse around the countryside, to wander along the freeways and by-ways and back roads until her nose, her eyes, and her intuition all tell her there is another shop just over there, over here, anywhere.

She loves to be at home in her sewing room, but every once in a while when we go on a trip to see the family or see the sights, she knows, I mean she *really* knows, if there is a fabric shop or quilt shop anywhere. And when she says, "Drive," I drive, and as I drive, she will raise her nose and lean her head and sniff for stash. If there's a shop within fifty miles of us, a hundred miles, she points me in the right direction.

13. Knots to You

"You were a Boy Scout," Darling Wife said.

"Yes, I was." She knew that before we were ever married. "That was fifty years ago," I said. She had something up her sleeve or under her collar or behind her back. She was up to something.

"And you learned some Boy Scout skills, didn't you?"

Now I was more than suspicious. She definitely wanted something. "I learned how to freeze while camping out in the snow with only a couple of blankets sewn together by my mother because we couldn't afford a sleeping bag. That was all I learned," I said. I was waiting.

"But you learned how to tie knots?"

"I never was any good at tying knots," I said. I wasn't going to fall for one of her tricks. I didn't know where she was going, but no doubt it involved me.

"But you could always untie knots," she said.

"They didn't give merit badges for untying knots," I said. I wasn't admitting to any skill that might later involve work.

"Well," she began. It was beginning.

"Well," I mimicked.

"Well, you know the ten-yard piece of fabric I bought yesterday for the quilt for our darling granddaughter?"

"Which ten yards? You bought ten yards of two kinds of fabric." I watched her carefully for any trick moves.

"Both ten yards. I just washed them and dried them."

"You want me to fold the fabric now?" She had given me that job one night long before when I was exhausted after driving one hundred fifty miles to a quilt shop and she needed "just a little favor."

"Well," she began. She hesitated and gave me her Look Number Seventeen, the one that says "You're so sweet to want to help."

"You want more from me than just folding twenty yards of hot fabric right out of the dryer, don't you?" Of course there was more.

"You are good at untying knots," she said.

"I think right now I might be better off untying that knot we tied thirty-eight years ago."

"And you're stronger than I am."

"That doesn't take much and that doesn't mean much," I said. I knew I was too far gone already, having continued this conversation too long. I should have run when she said "Boy Scout."

"It's in the cutting room," she said. She made a face of helplessness and pointed me that way.

What was in the cutting room, her old office where she had taught reading for many years before retirement, was twenty yards of fabric. Two pieces, each ten yards long. Washed and dried and hot and tied together. Somehow, perhaps under the guidance of a devil, the two pieces of fabric had braided together, the way those impossibly thin strings from wind chimes get forever entwined after the mildest breeze. The fabric was tangled, entangled, twisted, roped together, and there was no way in any way that I could see how to untangle them.

"How did you do this?" I hollered into the kitchen.

"A demon did it," she said.

"I would like to twist that demon's neck," I said, and I looked at the fabric in front of me and knew exactly how I would do that. The fabric, one piece printed with tiny blue rabbits, the other a garden of tiny flowers, both destined to be part of a quilt for our granddaughter's sixth birthday present—that fabric might never see the light of day again.

I tugged, I twisted, I untangled, I grunted, I turned and bent and spun around, and the fabric laughed at me. The two pieces were lovers, forever bound together by some magical spell.

"How's it coming?" she asked from the kitchen.

"It'scomingfineIalmosthaveit," I managed to get out, but somehow my words were now tied together as well. I looked at the fabric. I glared at it. I glowered. I spit into my hands and wrung them together and attacked, twisting, turning, churning, flipping, tossing, reversing, turning left and turning right. Twice I braided myself into the fabric. But I was making progress. Hadn't I once a long time before taken some Boy Scout oath to do my best to God, country and, some day, a quilting wife?

Half an hour later I had no muscles left in my body. My arms ached, my hands twitched, my fingers no longer existed. My shoulders were somewhere, but I had no idea where. I sat on the floor, my back pressed against the wall to keep my spine from cracking any further. But…but the fabric was separated and folded. "Ha!" I said to the vanquished 100 percent cotton.

"Honey, you finished yet?" She called from the kitchen.

"Finished? Finished?" Oh, yes, I was finished.

"Good. I'm ready to wash the rest of the fabric."

"There's more?" I asked in a whisper. I needed no answer. With a wife who sews, there's always more. But this time, I was going to insist that she cut all the fabric into four-inch squares before she washed. Maybe two-inch squares. One inch?

PART 4

14. The Right Stuff

She was going through the cupboard in the garage where we kept the office supplies. As a teacher, she had accumulated shelves full of supplies. As a retired teacher, she had boxed and stored them, moving them from one closet to another and finally into the garage as she replaced their spaces with stash. Now she was rummaging.

"Help me out here," she said as she moved aside reams of paper from the bottom shelf.

"You want to move the paper again so you can put in more stash here, too?"

"No, I need some paper."

"You have twenty reams of paper in front of you," I said to her. There was at least that much, though she had been using more and more lately, photocopying patterns and articles on quilting.

"They're all twenty-pound," she said. "They're not the right stuff. They rip too hard."

"They rip too hard?" I asked. I was in for another lesson in sewing English.

"They might rip out the stitches when I tear the paper away," she said, as if that explained everything to me.

"Go on," I said. I took two reams of paper from her as she handed them to me. I put them on the garage floor.

"When I finish making the square, I have to tear the paper," she said.

"Rip it or tear it? You just said you rip it."

"It's the same thing. I don't want to rip out the stitches."

"There are stitches in the paper?" An idea of what she was telling me began to form in my head, but I didn't want to even think she was in some way sewing the paper.

"There have to be stitches in the paper. I sew through the paper." She handed me two more reams of paper. I put them on the floor next to the first two.

"Are you making paper-doll clothes?" I guessed.

"No." She handed me two more reams. "Where are the eighteen-pounders?" she asked then.

"You're not talking about fish, are you?" I knew she wasn't. She was talking about the weight of the computer paper we used to use. But I didn't want to let her off too easily, not when she had me confused again.

"Paper-piecing," she said. "The twenty-pound is too thick. It tears hard, rips hard."

"Do you want to start over?" I asked.

"The new book came in the mail," she said. She pushed a ream of paper aside and reached far back into the cupboard.

"Which new book in the mail?"

"The new quilting book."

"Which new quilting book?" The post office was getting rich off the postage that stuck to the packages of books that had come since she had taken up quilting.

"The book on paper-piecing," she said. "I love it."

"You love a book on paper-piecing or you love paper-piecing?"

"Both," she said. She dropped a ream of paper and almost hit my toe, which was just an inch away from being paper-pieced, or -pierced, more likely. I jumped and backed away from the madwoman of paper. She paid no attention to the near-death of my toe and kept rummaging around.

"Is all of this paper too thick, too hard, too flat?" I asked.

"It's not too flat, Silly. It rips too hard," she said again. "And I need thinner, lighter paper."

"You need to sew on thin paper?" I was puzzled. I had looked at the cover of the paper-piecing book when she had opened the package three days before, but I had paid it no attention. My mistake. Now I had to go to paper-piecing school to keep up my end of the conversation.

"It's a technique for quilting that uses paper patterns. You sew the fabric through the paper, then rip the paper away."

"So that's what you've been doing for three days. I thought you were making a quilt."

"I was making a block," she said. She pulled herself out of the cupboard.

"For three days?"

"There's no old computer paper anywhere," she said.

"For three days?" I asked again. She had heard me.

"It's all backwards. I had to learn to do everything backwards," she said. "Have you ever tried sewing anything backwards?"

"Everything I sew is backwards," I admitted truthfully.

"Well, I had to learn out of the book and I kept getting everything backwards, but now I know how to do it, and I finished the block, and we have to go to the office-supply store and buy some thin paper so that I can rip the heck out of it."

"You learned how to do it in just three days?" I asked.

"Three long, hard days," she said. "Now can we go buy some paper?"

I looked down at the floor, the concrete covered in reams of thick, fat, obese, heavy twenty-pound paper. "What about this mess?"

"What about it?" She gave me her "I really have to get going on my paper-piecing project now" look. "You can put it back when we get back. It's not my fault we don't have the right kind of paper."

"You should have used skinny paper when you were teaching," I mumbled, but my words fell behind her. She was already back in the house getting ready to go shopping. "Then you would have some," I continued, but she was on her way to the office-supply store and what could be paper-piecing heaven if it had the right stuff for her to use. I ran after her. There was no guessing how much paper she would come back with on her own. When it comes to quilting....

15. Pick a Peck
of Paper

"Darn," she said, which meant much more than the word might otherwise imply.

"Problem?" I asked. I knew frustration when I heard it.

"Nobody told me it would be like this," she explained.

"Nobody told you what would be like what?" I asked.

"Taking off the paper."

Now, I have a fairly good grasp of the meaning of a lot of strange expressions in her quilting vocabulary, but I truly had not heard "taking off the paper" before. But then again, she was new to paper-piecing. And that was what she was doing. She told me that as she ran off after breakfast, leaving me to put away everything that breakfast entailed. She told me she was going into her sewing room to work on some paper-piecing block she found in the paper-piecing book she had been reading at the kitchen table during breakfast. She also said she "...didn't want to be disturbed while she was learning something new."

That had been two hours before. So when she said "darn" and "taking off the paper," I assumed it had something to do with the block she was constructing out of a lot of fabric or paper or thread or whatever.

"Two hours is a long time to make a block out of paper," I said. Perhaps she had been doing origami, folding the paper and fabric together and folding it again and again, but I was wrong.

"I finished the block a long time ago," she said. I watched her playing with a stiletto, attacking the paper and fabric she held down on top of the ironing board where she was standing. She made all her blocks standing, most of all because it was a good height for her, and, more importantly, because she had a bad back and could not sit too long at one time.

"Why are you attacking that block you say you finished a long time ago? It doesn't look like a block to me." I had seen her other blocks. They looked like blocks. This, whatever it was, looked like something that had gone through a shredder and had been pasted back together.

"It's upside-down," she said. She had put down the stiletto and was now using tweezers to "pluck" paper hairs from the skin of the block.

"You're playing Jaws with an upside-down block?" I asked. There was definitely something shark-like in her approach.

"I'm trying to take off the paper," she said.

"Doesn't it just tear off?" I asked. I knew the answer. She had been ripping paper all week, trying out every grade of paper, every weight of paper. She had finally settled on sheets of primary school news-print, which, after searching a dozen office-supply stores without success, we had found in the garage. She had reams of it, and though it was lined with faint blue lines, it copied in the copy machine and tore easily.

"It tears off in some places, but a lot of it gets stuck between the lines," she said. She lifted the clump of shredded whatever and showed it to me close-up. "There's not much space between where I stitched along the lines." She turned it over, and indeed I could see a gorgeous block, a small sailboat floating on a sea of blue.

"It's a great block, but why didn't you make it bigger?" I asked. I could see that it was indeed a block, but a very small block compared with the nine- and twelve-inch blocks she had made before.

"It's a four-inch block," she said. "It's for a wallhanging, not a big quilt, and it's bigger than some paper-pieced blocks. You should see the size of the miniature quilt blocks."

Stories by Popser

"But the little pieces are so little," I said. "You need to be Alice and drink some potion to make you tiny so you can cut and sew that." I didn't want to see a miniature anything.

"That's why it's so hard to take out some of the paper pieces."

"Why don't you leave them in?" Now that was a reasonable question to me, but I knew it might not be reasonable to her. But she surprised me.

"Some of the paper is left in. Many quilters leave the paper in. Some old quilts have paper that's been in them for years. It even makes the finished quilts warmer."

"So why are you working so hard?" I knew why. She was following directions.

"I'm just trying to follow the directions. I'm just learning."

"And the directions say to tear away all the paper?" I was catching on, I thought.

She nodded her head. "But it takes forever on some of this."

"Then find something else to do while you're doing it. Watch Oprah or something."

"I could listen, but I couldn't watch. I have to watch what I'm doing here."

"Why don't you listen to Oprah while you're doing that?"

"Oprah's not on until this afternoon."

"Then wait until you talk on the telephone to your sister. You could tear out the paper from a dozen blocks during just one conversation." I was gambling my life with that one. But she was attacking the paper again and paid no attention to me.

"I do kitchen chores when I talk to her."

"How about listening to the news?"

"I hate the news lately."

"You want some music to listen to?"

"Maybe some nice music."

"How about, 'It's only a paper moon'?"

16. Walking the Dog

Naturally, when I'm driving along the highway at seventy miles an hour, I keep my eyes on the road. That is why I didn't see what she was doing during the four-hour trip to see our son and his family. I knew she was busy. I saw the box of buttons she had brought into the car. She had bought a grab bag of buttons, and I assumed she was sorting them into small plastic bags. I was wrong.

"Did you get all the buttons sorted?" I asked when we reached our destination and were getting our bags out of the car.

"What buttons?" she asked.

"You brought the box of buttons," I said. "To sort," I added.

"I sorted them last week," she said.

"But you had that box?"

"No buttons," she said. "Yo-yos."

"Yo-yos?" What was she doing with toys, unless, of course, she had brought it for our granddaughter. Was she old enough at four-and-a-half for a yo-yo?

"You want to see them? I thought you wanted a break from my sewing."

"Wooden or plastic?" I asked. We both needed a break from her sewing. Visiting the family was a good break.

"Cotton."

"Are you in the same conversation I am?" I asked.

"You asked what the yo-yos were made out of."

"And?"

"I just told you."

"I never saw one made out of cotton. It wouldn't spin."

"Why would I want it to spin? I'll use thread so it doesn't spin."

"Thread? You can't use thread. You need special string so you can walk the dog. Thread will break."

"Are you in the same conversation I am?" she asked.

"Show me a cotton yo-yo," I answered.

"So you're interested in my sewing again."

"I'm interested in seeing you spin a cotton yo-yo."

"I'll get them," she said, and she moved back to the open door of the car and reached to the bottom of the front seat.

"How many did you bring?"

"I didn't bring any," she said.

"You said you brought yo-yos in the button box."

"I brought a needle and thread and the fabric for the yo-yos," she said as she closed the car door and came to my side. She carried a small two-handled shopping bag.

"I could do 'Rock the Baby' and 'Loop the Loop' and other stunts when I was a kid," I said. "And we had solid wooden yo-yos when I was a kid. Not even girls had cotton yo-yos."

"You're still doing tricks," she said. She reached into the bag and brought out a small scrap of flowered yellow fabric. "Here," she said, and she handed me the fabric.

"What's this?" I asked.

"A yo-yo," she said. Then she did an amazing thing. She reached into the bag and brought out a handful more of the scraps. She pushed them into my hands and then brought out some more. "Yo-yos," she said.

I looked at the growing pile in my hands. Each scrap was a small circle, sewed into the shape of a small blossom of some flower. Some were tiny and some were large and some were in-between. I looked more carefully. Each was sewn delicately, the rim folded over and stitched carefully. "Yo-yos?" I asked.

"That's what I was making."

"You made all these?"

"More," she said, and she opened the bag so I could look inside. There were about a billion little flowers in the bag.

"They look like flowers."

"Rosettes. They were very popular in the thirties. They made quilts out of these without any batting or backing. But they also can be used to decorate clothes. Or anything for that matter. I could decorate you. That would be an improvement."

"That might not be kind to my skin," I protested. I hoped she was kidding. I didn't need her sewing yo-yos anywhere on my body, improvement or not.

"I could use yo-yo puncture," she answered generously.

It was not a good time to encourage her. "You made them all on the trip," I said quickly. "I'm impressed. How did you sew them so fast?"

"How fast were you driving?"

"The speed limit. Seventy miles an hour."

"I made them at seventy miles an hour."

"Why are they called yo-yos?" I asked. Though each was round like a yo-yo, I saw no other similarity.

"What would you call them?" she asked.

"Bagels," I said.

"You're a yo-yo," she said, and she grabbed back all her little flowers and headed toward the house. "Bring in all the luggage," she said.

"You can eat bagels," I yelled after her though she was already in the house hugging our granddaughter. But I still had one of her yo-yos. I wondered if I attached a string to it whether I could still Walk the Dog.

17. Soap Story

I was in the shower, the water running, and I reached for the soap. There was only a sliver left, barely enough to wash my left elbow. I opened the shower door, leaned and dripped toward the drawer where we kept our extra soap, and reached for a new bar of Ivory. My hand came up empty.

I backed quickly into the shower, turned off the water, and haphazardly dried myself. As soon as I found some soap, I would return.

"Hon," I yelled loudly enough to be heard around the neighborhood. I stood partially draped in the large towel and waited for my Darling Wife to heed my call and run to my side.

Five or six years later, carrying two yards of wine-colored cotton fabric she had just removed from the dryer, she came sauntering in. "Yes, Dear," she said.

"We're out of soap," I said.

"Are you sure?" she asked.

"I'm sure," I said. "The drawer's empty. I thought we had some soap in there. Didn't we just buy some soap last week? There must be soap somewhere."

"I used it," she said. She casually began folding the piece of fabric.

"You were that dirty to use four bars of soap since last week?"

"Six," she said.

"Six?" I asked.

"I used six bars of soap."

"Well, that means either you're very, very clean or you are up to something." My bet was that she was up to something. I waited for her to confess.

"Pincushions," she said.

"Is that some kind of code?" I asked.

"Wait here," she said. Where was I going to go? My towel covered only so much. I sat on the bed as she left the room. I watched as she headed across the hall to her sewing room.

"Here," she said when she returned a moment later. She held something in her hand that was wrapped in blue fabric and looked like an upside-down hairbrush. The top of it was dotted by dozens of tiny yellow balls. Each ball topped a steel pin. "My new pincushion," she said.

"Pincushion?" Yes, it looked like a pincushion. But it was not round. Pincushions are supposed to be round and look like a cherry or strawberry. This was oblong, just about the size of... the size of a bar of soap.

"It's the wrapped bar of soap with some steel wool over it," she said. I gave her a very puzzled look. I had a good supply of puzzled looks and never ran out. I took the bar of soap, err, I mean, pincushion. I pulled out a quilting pin. I knew it was a quilting pin. It was long and thin and had a very sharp point. She was in the middle of another sewing frenzy. Hundreds of these midget daggers of steel had been all over the house. Now they seemed to be in my bar of soap.

"Steel wool?" I didn't use steel wool when I took a shower. I wasn't that dirty.

"The steel wool keeps the points sharp and the soap keeps them easy to use. Remember when the kids were babies and I kept all the diaper pins stuck in the bar of soap?"

"That was over thirty years ago," I said. Long before disposable diapers and Velcro and sticky tape, those slippery pins somehow found a way into our fingers when we changed the diapers, she much more than I. Ouch, I remembered.

"That doesn't explain why there's no soap in the soap drawer," I said, sticking to the point.

"I didn't plan to use it. I made some pincushions using all those small bars of motel soap we've collected on our trips. But when I started quilting, I started sneezing. I sneezed all over a yard of that nice corn-yellow fabric I just bought."

"You sneezed, so you stole the soap?"

"I didn't know why I was sneezing, but I sneezed only when I was quilting. So then…."

"Yes, go on. I'm listening to this strange alibi of yours for leaving your loving husband unwashed."

"All those little bars of soap were scented. That's why we put them in the guest bathroom and never used them."

"They made you sneeze and so you committed a third-rate burglary and plundered all the unscented Ivory."

"You got it, Babe," she said.

"But why six bars of soap?"

"I have lots of pins," she said. "I need two in the sewing room by the serger and sewing machines. I need one in the cutting room. I need two for basting the quilt." The queen-sized Amish quilt she was making was laid out on three banquet tables in the living room.

"That's five. What about the other one?"

"That's in case I lose one of the others."

"That makes sense. But what about my shower?" I asked.

"You can use the motel soap. Wait, I'll go get it for you."

She did, and I showered with the miniature soaps. I also sneezed. I sneezed because I'm also allergic to scented soap. But she wasn't sneezing. Oh, no. She had used six bars of soap to keep her pins sharp and easy to use and clean and very happy and she wasn't sneezing at all.

PART 5

18. My Story

"You always write about me. Why don't you write about yourself?" She was basting the edge of her Amish Quilt. She was very careful.

"I don't sew," I said.

"You used to sew," she said.

"That was many years ago."

"So?"

"All right, but just this once because you asked," I said, giving in easily. She flattened the edge of the quilt, which was spread out over three banquet tables.

"It doesn't have to be perfect," I said as she inspected each block. "Remember what all your sewing friends on the Net say. A tiny flaw makes you human. Quilters often leave a tiny flaw on purpose…."

"I make enough mistakes not to have to worry about that. Go away. Write your story."

My story!

My father was a tailor in Russia just after the Russian Revolution. When he was about twenty-one, he was successful enough to hire two apprentice tailors to help him. For that he was arrested by the police for exploiting labor. He was put in jail. Two nights later his girlfriend flirted with the guard while a male friend "borrowed" the keys to the cell and walked my father out of the jail house while the guard was otherwise "busy." My father moved to another town where he later met my mother, who was a woman's tailor. Some time later, my father bribed the local commissar to obtain a visa for him and my mother to come to America. My father went to work for a tailor in

Philadelphia, but he was soon successful enough to open his own shop. Eleven years later, I was born.

"How does that sound," I asked her.

"Are you going somewhere with that?"

"I needed some background."

"Well, snap it up. Get on with it. Put in some action." My director. I took her advice.

As my father worked in the shop all day and my mother was now a dressmaker and also worked in the shop all day, I spent my childhood around the shop. My best friends were the Singer my mother sewed on, a treadle machine with a leather belt that turned the wheel that made the needle go up and down (a wonder to a five-year-old) and my father's heavy-duty "man's machine." His Singer had an electric motor with a knee pedal and could sew through the heaviest material. I loved to hear the machines working and saw my parents as being lucky to sew all day long. I didn't know much at five.

But I soon learned to sew with a needle and spent time stitching scraps of cloth together, my mother's warning always in my ear not to put the needle through my eye (or any other part of my body). I did manage to thread my thumb twice.

By the age of nine I helped out in the shop and was allowed to open seams on men's pants with a razor blade to allow my father to take in the waist or let out the waist. "Don't cut yourself" was my constant warning. I could operate my mother's Singer by then, though I could barely reach the treadle. I could sew on buttons, though most of the time my job was to remove buttons from dresses before they were sent to the cleaner, where the delicate buttons might be destroyed. My mother sewed them back on. My parents were proud of my skills, but when it came to working on real clothes for customers, my parents forbade it. "You don't want to become a tailor. Go sit and read your books," they would tell me.

Yet I hungered to be like them, to make them proud, to show them what I could do after watching them work every day, after I practiced on thousands of scraps. I watched my mother and marveled that she could see a dress in a department-store window and come home and cut out a pattern from memory using old newspapers. I watched my father particularly because he could remake a man's suit from top to bottom to accommodate any man's changing size. I especially watched him alter my clothes, for I was the youngest of four sons and inherited almost all my clothes from my brothers. The clothes always started out too large, but they were always made to fit me. I watched how my father took in the waist, shortened the legs, and put in new buttons on the fly. (My childhood was zipperless.)

One day, I could no longer stand being an apprentice and wanted to achieve my manhood. Age nine was old enough. I needed to prove myself. So, I got up early in the morning and went down to the closed shop and found the pants my father had planned to shorten for me "in a day or two." I took them, along with scissors, needle and thread, a yardstick, tailor's chalk, some pins, and my dream of making my parents proud, upstairs to my parents' empty bedroom, while both of them were down eating breakfast. There on the far side of the bed, in hiding, I began my life as a tailor.

A long while later I heard my mother call me to breakfast, but I wasn't hungry. I was too involved in my sewing project. She called twice more and then gave up. She would later tell me, "You don't come to breakfast, you don't eat," but she would feed me anyway. Two hours from when I had begun, I was finished.

I had laid out my project, measured carefully, chalked lines across the material in the right places, pinned the cuffs (real cuffs, none of this modern sissy stuff), cut the material, folded and hemmed the cuffs, and puffed out my tiny chest with pride at what I had accomplished. All by myself! I was so proud, so eager, that I gathered the pants up, left all the mess on the floor behind me, and ran down the stairs to the shop where my father and mother sat at their machines, already well into their working day.

"So there you are," my mother said. And there I was, pants in hand, my face flushed, my heart beating in time with the treadle of my mother's machine as she pumped her legs up and down.

"Look," I said to her. "Pop, look!" I said to my father.

The machines stopped, the room became still. Time stopped. I displayed the pants, opening them up so the legs hung down in front of me, my creation unfurled. "Look," I said again.

They looked. There was a long moment of silence between them, and then it came. Though I expected exclamation, praise, admiration, and glory, there was instead tumultuous laughter. My mother and father, my mom and pop, both let out a cascade of laughter.

Puzzled, afraid, bewildered, I tried to explain. "I made the cuffs," I said.

"Yes, they are wonderful," my mother tried, but it was too late. Something was wrong. I looked at my parents and then down at the pants I held. One leg was shorter than the other. One leg was longer than the other.

I don't remember which leg was longer then, and though later I was able to learn patience and how to measure twice before cutting, and still later I learned to laugh at myself, I do remember that after the laughter stopped, my mother hugged me and my father patted my frail soul when he took the pants from my embarrassed hands and examined the cuffs and checked the stitching and said, "Almost perfect. Next time will be better."

There was going to be a next time, he promised, and I did learn to sew on his machine, though I never became a tailor. Twelve years later when I was in the army, I taught others how to hand-sew on their own buttons and make minor repairs to a split seam, but I never sewed much again after that.

"So, don't worry about a tiny flaw," I said to my darling wife after finishing "My Story." She had fully inspected her quilt and was smiling. "After all, when I made my first cuffs, there was a tiny flaw. It's a way of saying we're just human."

"How many inches shorter was one leg? You never told me."

"Two inches. Now can I write about you again?"

19. Getting the Hang of It

She called me into her sewing room as soon as I had finished lunch.

"I need a wall," she said, as I stepped into her town of Sew City.

"What?" I asked.

"I need another wall," she said.

"That's what I thought you said," I said.

"Then why did you ask me what I said?"

"I just wanted to make sure." Lately I have had to make sure about a lot of what she says to me. Our conversations have changed as she gets more and more into quilting, well beyond where either of us ever expected she would be. And I really thought I had been keeping up with her, but whenever I had thought that, I was usually wrong. That's why I asked her everything twice now. It was a matter of survival.

"So, what are you going to do about it?" she asked.

"About a wall?" I answered without hesitation.

"It's what I've been talking about," she said.

"I just wanted to be sure," I said.

"Now you can be sure."

"Why do you need another wall?" I asked. "Your sewing room already has four walls." I looked around the room. "One, two, three, four," I said. "If you count the closet you have seven walls."

"That's not enough," she said.

"That's enough to hold up the ceiling," I said. I knew no matter what I said, she would give me an explanation that was based entirely on her own brand of logic—quilting logic.

"It won't hold up my squares," she said.

"This has something to do with sewing and quilting, doesn't it?" I asked. It had to be a rhetorical question on my part. Of course it did. But she answered me anyway.

"I need it for my flannel sheet," she explained.

"You need a wall for a flannel sheet?"

"To hang the squares so I can get a good look at them." I knew she had just given me two answers, one ahead of my next question, which would have been to ask her why she had to hang squares, so I had to ask her something else.

"What about the flannel board I made you when you made your first quilt?"

"That was a lap quilt. I'm making more quilts. Some of them might be twin-size or queen-size."

"And you want another wall?"

"I need another wall," she said. "Have you looked around this house lately?"

"Of course, I've looked around this house lately." Of course. I knew where all the other walls had gone. They had disappeared. Vanished. Gone forever. Ever since she had read the book and started working her way through *Little Quilts All Through the House,* we had little quilts around the house. We had medium-size quilts around the house. We had wallhangings around the house. And I, of course, had to remove the pictures, the prints, the posters, and the shadow boxes, all so she could cover the walls. Now they were all used up and she wanted another one.

"Then you know I need to get some perspective on my squares. I have to be able to stand back and look at them, match colors, arrange and rearrange. I can't settle for the floor or the bed anymore. I do need a wall."

She didn't raise her voice. She didn't yell and demand and scream. But her soft words were just as effective as if she had used a bullhorn.

"Take down the family pictures," she said. She pointed to the only wall in the sewing room that didn't have shelves covered with all her stash and notions and thread.

"But, you love the photos there—" I began, but she gave me no time for objection.

"And move them into the cutting room. Then put up a queen-sized flannel sheet."

"You want the whole wall covered in flannel?" Of course she did.

"The whole wall," she said.

"And what about the photos?"

"Put them on the small wall over the cutting table."

"But you have the wallhanging you made last week hanging there."

"I took that down."

"But if you don't have any walls left, where will it go?" I protested for her sake. Did she know what she was doing?

She didn't answer but went instead to her sewing machine and picked up the wallhanging that had just recently hung in the cutting room. "I don't need another wall for this," she said.

"Are you going to just hold it up like that forever then?" I asked smartly.

Again, she didn't answer. She smiled and slowly turned the tiny quilt around to show me the back.

"What are you showing me?"

"I sewed magnets onto the back," she said brightly.

"Magnets?

"To hang on the refrigerator door."

"Of course. Magnets. Refrigerator. Door. Help!"

20. Error and Trial

*Y*ippee," she whispered.

"Yippee?" She was smiling a queen-sized smile.

"It's finished! Finished! Finished!"

"Why are you whispering?" I asked.

"It's a quilt shout," she said.

"You're really shouting?"

"Loud," she said. "Your quilt is done."

"You finished the queen-sized Amish Churn Dash quilt that you've been working on for ages?" I asked.

"Yes," she whispered.

"You're still whispering," I said. She should have been shouting.

"I don't want to brag," she said modestly.

"You should brag," I said. I'd brag. If I could cut a square out of one solid color, I'd brag.

"Even if it were perfect, I wouldn't brag."

"I can't hear you," I said. Her whispers were below my hearing threshold.

"Even if every stitch were perfect and every square were square and all the sashing were straight and the borders and the binding were absolutely flawless, I couldn't brag," she said. She spoke normally and I understood every word.

Now, what brought that on was my comment to her several weeks before when she was putting the top together. When she had reached the end of the first row of squares, she made the beginning quilter's mistake of asking me, the future recipient of the quilt, me the HH (Honest Husband), what I thought. "What do you think?" she asked.

"The third square is a little wider than the others," I said.

"Oh, you, what do you know," she said. It wasn't a question. It was a pout. More, it was the painful response to my answer, an answer based on my taking the Boy Scout oath fifty years before, that oath to tell the truth.

"It's not that bad," I said.

"Go make your own quilt," she said, and she upped and left the room.

It was three days later before she went back to the quilt. In the meantime she had sewn two outfits for our grandkids, made two embroidered bibs for a friend's new baby, and frowned at me whenever I said, "I'm sorry." And I said that a lot. For one thing, I'm not Pinocchio. For another thing, she is my Darling Wife. For a third thing, she was making the quilt for me. Most of all, I was sorry.

"I'm finishing the quilt," she said as she sat down at the sewing machine. "I'll finish it and if you don't want it because it's crooked, I'll give it to the first person who comes by and rings the doorbell and looks cold."

"Summer's coming," I said.

"It'll take until winter to finish this," she said. "Mistakes and all," she added under her breath.

"I don't see any mistakes," I said. The heck with a fifty-year-old oath.

"I'm just learning," she said. "Error and trial."

"Error and trial?"

"I made an error because I forgot how much the fabric could stretch when I was sewing the squares together, and asking you anything has been a trial."

"And tribulation," I said.

"Do you want me to finish this quilt or not?" she threatened.

"Yes," I said.

"Then get out of here and let me finish."

That was then and this was now, and the quilt was finished. She carried it into the bedroom. I followed quietly behind her. "Do you want this or not?" she asked as she held the folded quilt over the bed.

"I want it," I said.

"It has some errors in it," she said, testing my resolve.

"I won't see them," I said.

"You'll see them. You'll see that some of the sashing is crooked, some of the squares are not square, and some of the quilting is off a little. Every day for the rest of your life you'll see my errors. Can you live with that?"

"I want it," I said. I didn't see anything but perfection. She had worked long, long days the past week to finish the quilt.

So we spread the quilt out over the bed. The Amish design was gorgeous. The colors were a brilliant display of her hard work. The bed was no longer a bed. It was a base, a foundation for her quilt, our quilt. My quilt.

"I don't see any errors," I said honestly. So, maybe I am still a Boy Scout.

"And you'd better not," she said, "or the rest of your life will be a trial."

It was warming up in our town yesterday, but in our house the air conditioning was working well, and last night I slipped in under the quilt and slept very well indeed.

21. UFOs

What's a UFO?" she asked.

"An unidentified flying object," I answered.

"No, that couldn't be right. That's not a quilting definition."

"They have UFOs in quilting? Well, maybe it's because you're out in space so often when you're quilting."

"I won't even threaten you for that," she said. Obviously, she was serious about her question and had no time for humor.

"Maybe it means Ugly Fabrics Only."

"I think it has to do with some kind of objects," she said. "Quilters are always saying they don't have enough time to finish all their projects."

"That's not your problem. You never have time to do anything else."

She paid me no attention. "What words begin with U?"

"Up, Umbrella, Underwear. Maybe it's Underwear for Oldies," I suggested.

"No," she said, not taking the bait. "It has something to do with all kinds of sewing."

"Upset, Uniform, Uxorious," I offered.

"What's uxorious?"

"Excessively submissive or devoted to one's wife," I said. "The way you like me," I continued.

"Well, I should hope so," she said.

"How about Useful, Understand, Undulate? I like the way you undulate when you walk."

"Stick to the subject."

"Unknown, Unsung, Unlucky, Ubiquitous, Usual, Usury?"

"No, it's no use. There are too many words."

"How about Unfinished Objects?"

"What?"

"Maybe it has to do with projects you never finished."

"I never leave any projects unfinished."

"Yes, you do. You have a dozen drawers full."

"They're not UFOs," she said. "I'm working on all of them."

"You just said it."

"Said what?"

"UFO."

"Oh!"

"No, U-F-O. And you do have the hummingbird wallhanging and other projects you haven't finished."

"I'm still working on them."

"Then they're not finished."

"They're only unfinished when I don't plan to get back to them. I plan to finish them all. Sometimes I need more fabric or a notion or...."

"Or more time," I finished for her.

"That doesn't mean they're unfinished." She was stubborn.

"Then you can call them ICOs."

"What are they?"

"Incomplete Objects."

"Does that mean I'm still working on them?"

"That means you're still working on them." But very slowly, I thought to myself.

"Well, I don't give up, do I?"

"No, you never surrender. Now, how many ICOs do you think you have?"

"Only a few."

"Three? Ten? A hundred?"

"I don't have time to count them now. I have to finish what I'm working on."

"And what are you working on?"

"Oh, the hummingbird wallhanging, two other wallhangings, a crib quilt, a table runner, a pillow cover, and several paper-piecing projects."

"They're almost complete?"

"Almost," she said. She hesitated and continued. "Yes, of course. Well, a couple are just started, and a couple are just planned, but I'm going to do them. Now let me get back to work."

I let her get back to work. I'm going outside to look for real UFOs.

PART 6

WOOFLE

22. Then and Now

Sit still," I said.

"I am sitting still," she said.

"No, you're not sitting still," I said. "You want to leave."

"No, I don't want to leave."

"Then finish your lunch," I said.

"I am finished," she said.

"No, you're not," I said.

"I'm full," she said. "I have to go now."

"You want me to save the rest of your lunch or dump it?"

"Save it." With that our conversation was over. With that the kitchen chair was left empty. With that she ran to the sewing room, a woman on a mission, her sewing machine already humming before I took my next bite.

She had not always been like this. She used to stop and smell every flower in our neighborhood. She used to walk alongside me and talk to me about the earth, the sun, nature, our children and grandchildren, the neighbors, old friends, life in general. Now I wondered if there ever truly was a time when she didn't live, eat, drink, and breathe quilting. Oh, we still walked and talked, but somehow the conversations have changed. The leaves on the trees in our local park are a gallant green, and she notices them, of course, but where before she said, "I love the way the leaves look," she now says, "I think I'll put leaves around the border of the quilt." When she bends over to admire a row of tiny roses, she now says, "Miniature roses would make a great design for a miniature quilt."

When a cat crossed our path as we walked in our neighborhood, she used to say, "Remember the cat we had the first time I was pregnant?" Now she says, "I read about a woman in Rhode Island who had a cat that chewed up and ate ten yards of fabric the woman had left on the front porch as she carried groceries into her house. Then the cat coughed up colored cotton balls for a month."

"Do you mean hair balls?"

"Cotton balls," she insisted.

"What would they be if the cat chewed up a quilt?" I inquired.

"Quilt balls. What else?"

"Where did you read that?" I asked.

"In one of the quilting magazines."

"Sounds like the *National Quilting Inquirer*," I said.

Yes, we used to talk about the books and the magazines we read, the newspaper stories. But that was then and this is now. Lately, the books she reads are all about quilting. The magazines are overwhelmingly quilting. And though she does keep abreast of current events and watch the evening news, she is quick to wonder aloud how the fabric on the newscaster's dress could be cut into pieces to make a Colorado Star or a Drunkard's Path. Actually, she does listen to the news as she quilts. And when she learned from the national weather report that a cooling spell was just around the corner, she hoped that there were enough warm quilts for every bed in every state where the temperature drops below fifty degrees. Then she mused aloud, "I wonder what kind of quilts they make in Canada?" She wants to go there to find out.

She also talks of visiting all 50 states. I suspect that she has hidden away somewhere a list of all the quilting shops in each state. I'll be very wary when she gets that look in her eye and says, "Honey, let's go for a ride," as she points on the map to Paducah, Kentucky, which is just about two thousand miles from our kitchen.

I finished lunch, cleaned up for both of us, and went to get my Darling Wife. It was time to shop for food. Usually she would rather organize her stash of fabric than shop for food, and I would go alone, but she had asked to go along this time to get out of the house and away from making bias strips for her unicorn appliqué.

"Sometimes, I need a break," she had said to me earlier.

Sometimes she did need a break, but to me a break meant getting her away from herself, getting her away from the house, getting her away from the rotary cutter, away from her thinking about cutting the bed sheets into a thousand tiny triangles and squares and strips. No way! And, of course, five minutes into the drive to the market she began getting anxious to go back home. Her anxiety showed up as she started to tap the dashboard.

"Everything all right?" I asked. She squirmed on the seat.

"How much shopping do we have to do?" she asked.

"Only as much as you want," I said.

"We need only a few things," she said. She tapped and tapped.

"All right," I agreed. Actually we needed a lot of things, and shopping would take at least an hour, but I understood her tapping, her squirming.

So, I was not surprised when we were in the market only five minutes and she said, "I have what we need." She had put three apples in the shopping cart.

"Nothing else?" I asked. I knew there would be nothing else. She was looking intently down into the cart.

"Do you think this would make a good quilting design?" she asked.

"What?"

"This cart. Look at the way it's made. Look at the chrome-plated design."

"It's just a shopping cart," I said.

"Well, it has a nice design. Maybe I can make a wallhanging that looks like a shopping cart and appliqué some apples into it." She was very intent as she examined the cart.

"I'll drop you off home and you can go back to your ironing board or your sewing machine or your stash collection," I said.

"But what about the shopping?" she asked. She used her fingers to measure the mesh of the cart.

"I'll come back and do the shopping," I said.

"You don't mind?"

"Not if you have a lot of cutting or piecing or sewing or quilting to do."

"I just have to finish a few things," she said. "Then we can go for a walk later when you come back from shopping."

"A walk?"

"Of course. We can take a nice walk and look at all the flowers in the neighborhood. Don't you ever notice how many flowers are in bloom right now?"

"Sounds fine to me," I said. "We might even take the time to smell them," I added.

23. Yip-Yap

As we drove into the driveway in front of our house, she became more and more eager to be inside.

"I'm eager to be inside," she said.

"I never would have guessed," I said.

"Don't get smart. You know what's happening, don't you?"

"I know you've been away from your quilt projects for three days."

"It's not me," she said.

"It's not?" I suggested and asked at the same time. During the time we were away, we had visited a quilt show on California's central coast. That visit had kept her calm, happy, cool, in command. But as we drove the two hundred sixty miles home, the car full of new fabric, new projects, paper-piecing kits, appliqué kits, and new notions for quilting, she ached to be home, to get back to her quilting.

"It's the projects," she said. As the car rolled to a stop, her hand was already moving toward the release of her seat belt.

"The car's still moving," I said. I braked and moved to pull up the emergency brake and turn off the ignition.

"They need me," she said.

"Your projects need you?" I asked. She already had her door open.

"Can't you hear it?"

"Hear what?" I asked. I knew immediately she heard something. She had a strange grip on reality when it came to her quilting.

"All the yipping and yapping," she said. "They know I'm home and they all want my attention."

"We don't have dogs," I said, though the neighborhood had dogs, but they mostly growled and barked.

"Not the dogs," she said as she left the car.

"What about the packages, the luggage, all your quilting stuff?" I said, as she began to pick up speed as she went up the pathway to the house. As for the "stuff" she bought, what else would I call it? How else do I explain all the quilting paraphernalia tucked away in too many packages?

"You bring them in," she said.

I brought in the luggage and the packages and the ice chest and the trash bag and cleaned out the car. During the whole time I struggled and carried and lifted and packed and toted, she was busy running around the house.

"Are you all right?" I asked on one of our chance encounters in the hallway.

"They're all yelling to be first," she said cryptically.

"Is that some code?" I asked her. I didn't really have to know her codes. Quilters talk in mysterious ways, and I long ago just assumed that anything she said that I didn't understand had to do with quilting.

But she was gone in a flash toward her cutting room. Minutes later, when she buzzed by me again, I tackled her. "Yelling what?" I asked. "I thought they were yipping and yapping." I held her tight so she wouldn't escape.

"Are you deaf?" she said. It's true I have lost some of my hearing of high-pitched sounds, so yipping sounds might be beyond my hearing threshold, but I thought I should still be able to hear yapping.

I strained to hear. "Nothing," I said. She was squirming to get free of my husbandly hold.

"You're not a quilter," she said. "Quilters hear those sounds."

"I'm the Darling Spouse of a quilter," I said. "I should be able to hear a few squeaks and squeals."

"They're yipping and yapping all over the house," she said as she finally pushed me back and broke away. "They need my attention," she said.

"Fabrics don't yip," I said. "Quilts don't yap," I said. "Projects don't make any sound humans can hear," I said, but she was long gone.

I unpacked and put everything away and sighed. I left her packages, her bundles, her bags, and her boxes all in the hall. She would get to them before I ever saw her again, I knew.

But I was wrong. She was back in a moment. She had a strange look on her face. "What?" I asked. "Did they stop their yipping and yapping now that you're back?"

"They're louder than ever," she said.

"You couldn't calm them down?" I asked. Why was I in this conversation?

"It's not me," she said, her face showing anxiety. "They're arguing over who gets to go first."

"Who goes first?" I was in an Abbott and Costello routine.

"I have all these projects waiting and now each one wants to go first. I can't decide which one to do first, and they all want to be first. I need your help."

"My help? What can I do?"

"You decide which one I should do first."

"How many are there?"

"Ten, twenty, dozens and dozens. I don't know."

"Which one are you in the mood to do?"

"All of them. I want to do every single one."

"But which one do you really want to do now?"

"I don't know. Maybe the Cheyenne Star, maybe the baby quilt, maybe the unicorn appliqué, maybe the Drunkard's Path, maybe the table runner, maybe the potholder. I just don't know."

"How about a lottery?" I asked. "Pick straws? Cut the cards? Roll the dice? Spin the bottle?"

"A lottery might work," she said.

So we had a lottery. She put the names of all her projects into a bucket (there were a lot of names and it was a big bucket), and I blindfolded her, spun her around three times, recited a quilter's prayer, and led her hand to the bucket. She pulled out a slip of paper.

I took the paper and read it. "Well?" she asked as she removed her blindfold.

"Well, it says here…," I began.

"Tell me," she said firmly. Very firmly.

"Grandmother's Flower Garden," I said. "Now go tell the other projects," I said. "I don't want any more yipping or yapping."

"What are you talking about?" she said. Now the house was suddenly quiet.

"Nothing. Nothing at all," I answered. And that is how she chose her new quilt project.

24. Color Me Shy

We had just come from Quilt in a Day and Calico Station in San Marcos, and now we were in JoJo's Calico Courtyard, a recommended quilt shop in Temecula, all in Southern California. This was already our third quilt shop that morning. I was standing in line behind three women who were having fabric cut. The woman behind the counter was working quickly when she looked up at me. I was standing there holding a small package, an appliqué kit for a quilt my Darling Wife had decided she needed more than anything in the world just then. That our car was already bulging didn't matter. That she had told me twice before that morning she needed something else "more than anything in the world," didn't matter. That one more package, even one this small and weighing only a few ounces, didn't matter either. What mattered was that I was waiting to pay and that there were three women ahead of me, each one waiting, no doubt, to have dozens of bolts of fabric cut into quarter yards.

I was in no great hurry, for Darling Wife was still wandering the store. Though our charge card was already beyond its quilting limit, that also didn't matter. What mattered was buying something in every quilt shop in America. I think she kept extra charge cards hidden somewhere on her body, just in case.

As I stood there, I expected to wait a couple of days in line, but just then the woman directly in front of me turned and saw me behind her. She looked me up and down, looked at the one item I was going to buy, and nodded her head up and down. Then she turned back to the women in front of her.

"There's a man in here," she said. It took only a second before the woman in front of her turned to see me. I smiled.

"There's a man in here," the woman in front of the woman in front of me said. They all turned to look at me. The woman cutting the fabric stopped in mid-snip and looked at me. I smiled at all of them, sharing my smile as each one looked me up and down.

"He looks so uncomfortable," the first woman said with great compassion in her voice, as if I were homeless and she had come across me lying in front of the quilt store with my hand held out for a donation of food or a fat eighth.

"It's hard for a man to be in here with all these women," said the second woman.

"Morning," I said in my friendliest voice. I looked around. In addition to my wife, there were ten other women roaming the aisles, feeling the fabric, picking through the patterns and quilting books.

"Men have a terrible time in quilting shops, don't they?" asked the third woman. The other two looked me up and down again and nodded in agreement.

"We should let him go first," said a new woman who came up behind me in line and spoke around me to the others.

"He must be terribly nervous," said the one directly in front of the one directly in front of me.

"He can go first," she said, and she moved aside. The woman in front of me moved aside. The woman at the head of the line moved aside.

"Go on. We know how you feel," they all said.

Now, I was brought up in an age of politeness. I knew women went first. I knew women walked on the inside away from the curb. I knew all about courtesy. So, I hesitated. But the woman behind me pushed me toward the front of the line. "Go on," she whispered.

I went to the front of the line and paid. "Come back," the owner said as she put my purchase in a bag.

"I will," I said with a wink. I went over to the bookrack and showed my Darling Wife that the package was already paid for.

"That was fast," she said. I sensed some disappointment. No doubt she hoped it would take me all day so she could browse and maybe, just maybe, find something she really needed more than anything else in the world.

"I'm very uncomfortable in a quilting shop with all these women around," I said.

"What?"

"That's what they said," I said as I turned her toward the women at the counter. "They all let me go ahead."

"If they only knew," she said. And she smiled and we left the shop.

Now, in the months since she took up quilting, we have been in dozens of quilting shops and fabric shops. In many of them, people looked at me and, no doubt, puzzled over my presence. No doubt people wondered how my Darling Wife could stand having a man along when *she* went shopping for fabric. Some even asked her that question.

"Why doesn't he wait outside with the other men?" she was asked at one chain fabric store by a woman who saw me looking closely at some fabric, perhaps too closely, as if she suspected I might have a choice in what Darling Wife bought. On the way into the store, I had seen a small group of men. I assumed they were husbands of quilters, tied up at some imaginary hitching post.

"Isn't this embarrassing for him?" my wife was asked in a quilt shop in Hawaii.

"Doesn't he get in the way?" another asked as we went up and down the aisles at a quilt shop in Kentucky.

Oh, occasionally there was a look of surprise and a smile as a woman might say, "It's so nice that you have your husband to help you carry everything."

When I called one quilt shop to ask why there had been no bill with my wife's order, I was reluctantly told by the owner, "Oh, well, you see, some women don't want their husbands to know how much they spend on fabric."

Oh, I know there are men who quilt and other men who accompany their wives quite happily and men who help with the decisions that their wives make. But I also know there are men who would rather have rabies than be found in a quilt shop. I'm just not one of them.

"I think we should stop in one more shop on the way home, maybe 5 Heart Quilts in Tehachapi," my Darling Wife said as we approached our car.

I made a face. "What are you making a face for? You like quilt shops."

"I'm practicing looking embarrassed," I said.

"You don't look embarrassed. You look as if you had rabies."

"Well, if I can look embarrassed," I said, as I practiced blushing, "maybe I can get to go to the head of the line again. Look at how much time we'd save, and we could visit twice as many quilt shops."

She looked at my face carefully. "A little redder," she said.

25. Silver Threads

was about to put a slice of tomato into my tuna sandwich when I spotted it. There, clinging to the surface of the tomato, was a blue thread. "What's this?" I asked my Darling Wife as I plucked the thread free and held it up for her to see.

She reached over for the thread and looked at it closely. "Kona cotton," she said. "Blue. From the half yard I was cutting."

"It's a piece of thread unraveled from a piece of fabric," I said. "Why was it attached to my slice of tomato?" I asked. How she could identify it as Kona cotton, I would never understand.

"Sometimes that happens," she said.

"I could have swallowed that, and when ER doctors X-rayed me, they would have said I had a threadworm," I protested.

"It wouldn't kill you," she said, and she put the piece of thread down on the side of her plate and continued eating her own sandwich.

"One wouldn't kill me," I said, "but there's never just one, is there?"

"Finish making your sandwich, Dear," she said.

I added cheese to my sandwich, but I was careful. Too many strange things had been happening in our house the past few months. As longer days were fast approaching, I began to wonder if we didn't have quilting spirits celebrating the summer solstice circulating throughout our house.

"What about the trail of three-and-a-quarter-inch triangles I found going from the hall to the bathroom last week?" I asked.

"They were for the paper-pieced sailboat," she said. "I wondered where they had gone."

"Probably looking for a large body of water," I said.

"Sometimes a piece gets lost," she said.

"What about the square I found under the blanket when I rolled over in bed yesterday morning?"

"Mary's Flower Garden," she answered quickly before her next bite of sandwich. "I was looking for that."

"And last Sunday when I went to clean off the counter and almost used the nine-patch square that was wrapped around the paper towels by the sink?"

"I don't remember that," she said innocently.

"Then how about the strip of marbled red fabric in the *TV Guide*?"

"That was so I could find Thursday's listing for 'Simply Quilts.'"

"And the morning I found my white T-shirts were pink and my shorts stuffed with fat quarters?"

"I forgot your underclothes were in there when I pre-washed the fat quarters. That one piece of batik ran a little red." She looked up at me. "Anything else?"

"Since you're asking, yes. Why was there a paper-piecing pattern for the perfume bottle in the refrigerator?" I had found it by the milk.

"I was putting back the milk," she said. "I must have left the pattern there by mistake. Thanks for finding it for me."

"That's it? A mistake? Thanks for finding it?"

"I was looking all over for it."

"Were you also looking all over for the rotary cutter?" I had found that in the medicine cabinet when I discovered my razor was missing three days before.

"You know where that is? I've been looking for that for days."

"I tried to trim my beard with it but it didn't work," I said. I finished making my sandwich and took a small bite, my tongue alert for thread.

"I hope you didn't ruin the blade," she said.

"Talking about blades," I said, remembering all too well how my backside was almost pierced by the tip of her seam ripper when I accidentally sat down on it. "I put your seam ripper back in your sewing room." I wouldn't ask her how it got into the living room. I was only glad that it hadn't been the new stiletto she bought for her appliqués.

"I made that star square and attached one of the pieces backwards. Do you know how hard it is to rip out those tight stitches?"

"I know how hard it is to dig down into the shower drain to clean out the clog from all the fibers and thread and lint stuck down there after your shower last Tuesday."

"I worked on three projects that day. I'm a quilter. Quilters some-times get a thread stuck on their clothes or in their hair. Do you want to hear about the grass clippings and pine needles and leaves your feet dragged in after you raked the front lawn?"

"There was only one leaf, one pine needle, one blade of grass," I said in my defense. "You drag threads and bits of fabric and pieces of your projects all through this house. Do you remember the piece of interfacing you just 'accidentally' ironed onto my pants?"

"Hah!"

"What's with this 'Hah!'?"

"That was my last piece of interfacing. I'm all out and I need to buy some more."

"I'll go get my pants…."

"And a yard of…."

"I'll stop if you stop," I said.

"All right, but I do have to go to the quilt shop."

"Looking like that?" I asked as I looked at her.

"Looking like what?"

"Your hair is full of thread," I said.

"Thread?" She ran her hand through her hair.

"Lots of thread," I said.

"What color?" she asked. I reached for one of the threads and handed it to her. "Metallic silver," she said. "I'm learning how to use metallic thread."

"It's in your hair," I said.

"How's it look?" she asked.

"Better there than it would look on a slice of tomato."

"Better there than it would look stuffed down your throat?" she asked, as she used her fingers to comb more thread out of her hair.

"Looks good," I said. "Yep, looks very good," I agreed. Well, she is my Darling Wife and I have many sandwiches left to eat before I sleep. Thread-free sandwiches, I hope.

26. Dang!

"Dang it," she said.

"What was that?" I asked as I passed by the door to her sewing room.

"Dang, dart, dewlap," she said.

"Are you all right?" I asked. I wondered if I had heard her right.

"The needle just broke," she said in explanation.

"And that upset you?"

"I'm right in the middle of finishing the quilt binding," she said. She was obviously annoyed.

"So, what's with the 'Dang it'?" I have heard more colorful words from her when she was annoyed.

"I was watching my language."

"You were watching your language?"

"I just said that," she said. She was taking out the broken needle from the machine. "Oh, feedle!" she said.

"Now what?" Feedle?

"I can't find the piece that broke off the needle. I think it fell down onto the floor. I'll never find it until I'm barefoot."

"That's the way I find lost thumb tacks," I said helpfully.

"Drat," she said. "I'll never get this finished."

"'Dang,' 'feedle,' 'drat'? What's with your new vocabulary?" She knew much better words for annoyance and frustration and letdown.

"I needed new words. The other words are all so coarse and vulgar."

"They're good old American words," I said in mild protest.

"Old and obscene," she said. "They just sound rotten."

"But we need words to shout when our car doesn't start in the morning or when the coffee burns our tongues or the IRS sends us a letter. What would you say if you were to step on that needle in the middle of the night when you get up because you finally remember where you'd left the quilt magazine that you had lost and you suddenly need it at two AM?"

"Scump," she said.

"'Scump'?" Did I hear her right?

"Oh, all right. Fepperplatz."

"Honey, Dear, are you all right?" I asked, just slightly concerned that she might have broken more than the needle. This was a woman who, in more than thirty years of teaching, had heard every foul word ever spoken. "'Fepperplatz'?"

"I have to be careful what I say," she said. "I have new words."

I looked around the room. I didn't see anyone there. "Why do you have to be careful?" I asked. I always ask good questions like that.

"I don't want to offend the sewing machine," she said.

"The sewing machine? You don't want to offend the sewing machine?" Had I heard her correctly? Or did I have wax in my ears?

"It's less than a year old, and it's worked perfectly so far. It's still so young, and I don't want to upset it."

"Why do you think it will get upset if you say something that's not nice in polite society?"

"It just does. I didn't attach the border to the quilt just right the other day, and I got mad and said something rotten, and then the machine slowed down and stopped. I apologized and it went back to work."

"You apologized to a sewing machine?"

"I promised I wouldn't say anything bad anymore."

"So, you use nicer words?"

"Yes," she said. She finished replacing the needle and threaded it and got ready to work on the quilt again. I looked at the machine to see if it was content.

"What kinds of words?" Maybe I could write a new dictionary.

"When I burn something with the iron, I say rump or frample," she said with a soft song in her voice. I think she was caressing the machine at the same time.

"What if you accidentally threw out the last yard of fabric you needed for your new Friendship Star quilt binding after working forty-eight hours straight to get the quilt finished and there was no more fabric in the world that you could replace it with."

"I never throw out any fabric," she said. "I'm doing the binding now."

"But if you did?"

"Blankety doop," she said.

"And if you ran a needle through your finger?" She had to lose control sometime.

"I haven't done that since I was in junior high."

"But if it happened again. What would you say?"

"Heck's peck! I'd say it loud, too."

"Just so you wouldn't upset the sewing machine?"

"And the quilt, too."

"They might get their feelings hurt?"

"Words can be cruel," she said. She began sewing. The telephone rang in the other room.

"I'll be back to hear some more," I said. I turned to leave the room, and in my bewilderment at what my Darling Wife had just told me, I bumped into the doorframe. "Oh, forkle," I said, my head throbbing from the collision.

"Are you all right?" my wife asked with deep concern.

"I'm all right," I said as I rubbed my head. But what I really wanted to say was, "Gush, darn, doofle trup."

27. Project 39

We were in yet another quilting shop waiting for her quilting supplies to be packed up in three large shopping bags. She was excited about the new fabric, the new bobbin case, the new stencils, the new quilting thread, the new scissors, and too much else. I was excited about bankruptcy.

"Look at this," she said to me as she wandered over toward a wall of quilts on display. Since she had taken up quilting months before, we had spent what seemed like ninety-eight percent of our waking hours looking at quilts. Every sewing or quilting store we visited had quilts. When we went to Wal-Mart for some aspirin, she somehow found out it had quilts hanging in the fabric section. When we went to a gas station in Lancaster, Pennsylvania, there was a quilt hanging over a motor-oil display. All God's children, it seemed, either made or had quilts.

"Look at what?" I asked. I was already looking in my checkbook to see if I would ever have a positive balance again.

"This quilt," she said as she pointed to a small quilt hanging on the wall of the shop, one among many. Too many. I looked. The quilt had a lot of pointy things and a lot of square things and some triangular things and it was very colorful. It was beautiful, but I wasn't going to tell her that. She'd want to make one just like it.

"Um, yes, very nice," I said, trying to turn away and divert her attention toward my checkbook and the fact that she had spent all our food money for the next three years.

"I'm going to make one like it," she said, not easily diverted from anything having to do with her new passion in life.

"I thought you were going to make that one over there that looks like a blue checkerboard," I said, pointing to a blue-and-white quilt that looked like a checkerboard.

"I am," she said. She gave me a look that asked me why I didn't understand her passion to make more than one quilt.

"But you want to make that quilt as well?"

"Lots of quilts," she said. It was her mantra. She had already completed six quilts, five wallhangings, and started a dozen more of both. PIP's she called them. Projects In Progress. She was a human quilt factory.

"Are you ready to go now?" I asked her, as I grabbed the three bags. I had to get her out of there before she lost all control. But she did not answer. In a blink she had disappeared. I looked around and saw her at another display at the back of the store. Darn, she was fast. I put down the bags and hurried over to her. I wondered if there was some kind of blinders I could have her put on when we went into a quilting shop. Just in and out. Buy the one item she needed and scoot her out into the real world. I have a dream!

"Look at this," she said.

"Do I have to?" Of course. I looked at a quilted carry-all, a large bag that looked like a sleeping bag for a pet monkey. We didn't have a monkey. We didn't need the bag. "You don't need a bag," I said. "We have no more money for a bag. We will never again have any money for a bag."

"I'm not going to buy it," she said in her "exasperated-with-me" kind of way. "I'm going to make one."

"I thought you were going to make the quilt we just looked at."

"I am. I'm going to quilt a lot of things. There are a lot of things to quilt."

"But you have all those other projects you said you were going to make, don't you?" Of course she did.

"I'll make them all," she said.

"You don't have time to make them all," I said. She looked at me. She just kept on looking at me. "Do you?"

"I'm very organized," she said. "I'll make time. Now, write the bag down as thirty-nine."

"What?"

"Project thirty-nine," she said.

"What's thirty-nine?" I was very confused just then. First of all I had no paper. I had no pencil. I had no idea what she was talking about.

"To add to my list of projects. I already have a quilt like the one on the wall down as project twenty-two, so you don't have to write it down again. This is project thirty-nine."

"You have a list of projects? I never saw any list."

"I have a list at home. Otherwise I couldn't remember all the projects I have to do. Now I have to add these to the lists, and I don't want to forget."

"That's understandable," I said. "You plan to do thirty-nine projects."

"You got it, Babe."

"And what if you see something else you like?" Just what if?

"Then that would be project forty." Or fifty or sixty, I thought.

I looked back to the counter where her three full bags sat. "We should get your packages before someone takes them," I said. I took her hand and dragged her back toward the counter. Thank goodness she came with me. Maybe now she wouldn't think of any more projects.

"Now, look at that," she said as she suddenly stopped by a table covered with new fabrics. My arm stopped as well, stretched about three feet longer than it had been.

"Nice table," I said. She didn't want any more fabric, did she?

"Remind me to get some new colors," she commanded. "Add it to the list."

"What list?" I asked. I hoped she had forgotten.

"You did write down the carry-all as project thirty-nine, didn't you?" she asked. She is not an easily distracted woman. I went to the counter, borrowed a pencil, begged a piece of paper, and wrote down what she told me to write down, project thirty-nine and new colors.

"Don't lose the paper," she said.

I would never think of it.

28. When I'm 164

"Will you still love me?" she asked out of the blue, even though it was a very cloudy day and we were caught in a drizzle as we came home from the library.

"Yes, I still love you," I said.

"I don't mean now," she said as the drizzle became rain and her words were wet.

"Whenever," I said, as I wiped rain from my glasses so I could see to unlock the front door. I opened the door and she damply squished past me into the house. I followed her into the house and into the bathroom where we grabbed for towels and wiped ourselves dry before she spoke again.

"'Whenever' is not an answer," she said as she pulled the towel from her head.

Since we had been in the house a busy five minutes spent getting dry, I had forgotten our walking-in-the-rain conversation. "Ask me again," I said. I assumed she had asked me a question and I had probably given her a wrong answer.

"I asked you," she said as she casually flicked her towel at me, "if you will still love me."

"When?" I asked. She flicked the towel again, harder and better aimed.

"When I'm one hundred sixty-four," she said.

"Ouch," I said. "Don't you mean sixty-four?" Listening to the Beatles years before, we had both pledged our hearts at least that long. I didn't remember anything about quilt projects.

"No, I mean one hundred sixty-four."

"All right," I said. I'm easy, but I'm also curious. "Do we plan to be around that long?" I asked.

"We have to be if you want me to finish," she said.

"Finish?" I caught the towel before it flicked again and moved down the hallway to the kitchen. She followed me without saying a word. When I opened the refrigerator, she answered.

"Your quilt," she said.

"I have a quilt," I said.

"I know you have a quilt. But you said you liked the Friendship Star quilt, so I have to make one for you."

"Is there a problem that needs to be solved here?" I asked. "I don't need a new quilt."

"I started it," she said. I reached for the bowl of salad on the top shelf.

"You started what?" I asked. I put the bowl of salad on the kitchen counter.

"I started your quilt, but I won't be able to finish it right away," she said.

"That's all right," I said. I went back to the refrigerator for the salad dressing.

"I finished forty squares already," she said.

"You did?"

"I need a lot more than that," she said.

"You do?" I found the salad dressing hidden behind the large economy-size ketchup bottle.

"But I have too many other projects I want to do, too," she said. "Maybe I can use the squares in a different project. That way they won't have to wait."

"You just said they were for my quilt," I protested. I wanted those squares to hang around as long as I did.

"I can make others. In the meantime, I can use them in some gift quilts…."

I stopped her. "Such as?" I asked pointedly.

"Such as that housewarming quilt I plan to make or the table runners or the pot holders."

"You'd give away my squares?" Where was her loyalty?

"Maybe not," she said. She paused and looked at me. I looked back. "All right, I'll save them for you. It's just that there are so many quilts I want to make." She was wistful. I knew that look.

"You have a lot of quilts on your list," I confirmed. Were all quilters' lists endless? Her list was friends with eternity.

"You don't mind waiting?"

"How long?" I reached into the freezer for some bread to go with the salad.

"A long time," she said.

"All right," I agreed. "I won't mind waiting."

"More than a hundred years," she added.

"That is a long time," I said, thinking it through. The bread would be well thawed out by then.

"Will you still love me?"

"Until you finish my quilt?"

"I'll be one hundred sixty-four," she said.

"That's very old," I said. Would I need a quilt then?

"I have to finish all the other projects," she said.

"You have that many projects?" Of course she did. She was long past her list of thirty-nine projects. Every time she opened a quilting magazine she added a new project. Every trip to a quilt shop brought a new project or two. One trip to a quilt show can add a dozen projects. Another project and blood banks won't call her any more because of her having too high a quilt-project count in her blood. "I know someone who only made one quilt in her whole life," I added. It was a fib, a little white lie, but I had to do something to discourage her from taking on any more projects.

"Who was that?" she asked.

"It was in some quilt magazine," I said, compounding my chicanery.

"You're just making that up. But it doesn't matter. I am going to keep on quilting for a long time. So, just tell me now, will you still care for me when I'm an old, old woman who can barely see the quilt, let alone the sewing machine; when I'm shriveled down into nothing with age, still working away hour after hour, day after day, squinting at every stitch just to finish your quilt?"

"Absolutely," I said. I know which side of my bread the butter's on. Bread! I went back into the refrigerator for the butter.

"I just wanted to know," she said.

"Three thousand and one," I said.

"What?"

"Will you still love me until the next millennium?"

"What will take you that long to finish?" she asked.

"Getting my dinner," I said.

"Don't be silly."

"Love isn't silly," I said.

"You're right," she said. Then she paused, looked at me, and said, "Do you want some hearts on your quilt?"

"Yes, hearts," I said. "I think I want lots of hearts." I will need them all when I'm one hundred sixty-four.

29. Dust Rags

*W*hat are you doing?" she asked, alarm in her voice.

"Dusting off the window sills," I said. She should have been cheering.

"What are you using for a dust rag?" she asked, her eyes attached to the rag I held.

"Just a rag," I said innocently. But her look found me guilty of some grave offense.

"Just a rag?" she asked as she grabbed the rag and shook it out to see what it was. As the rag and I had been working hard just moments before, she also shook out sixteen tons of dust. "This was the beginning of a new quilt!" she exclaimed. I'm not always sure what an exclamation sounds like, but she sounded as if she were really exclaiming.

"What?" I said, trying to get back to innocence.

"Where did you get this?" she asked. She looked it over carefully. She tried to straighten out some of the wrinkles. It didn't look like anything but a rag, a very dirty rag.

"In the back of the hall closet where you keep all the rags," I said.

"I don't keep any rags back there," she said, and before I could answer she darted off down the hall to the closet. I followed cautiously.

"There's a small pile of rags," I said. "You have small piles of them in the back of all the closets," I added.

"They're not rags," she said. "They're just...." Her voice trailed off. She pulled out several of the "rags."

"They're just what?" I asked. When she didn't reply immediately, I became insistent. "Just what are they?"

"Mistakes," she said softly, more to herself. "They're just mistakes I made while learning how to quilt. See," she said, showing me the rag she held. It was a nine-inch square with what was supposed to be a Flying Geese design. It looked more like a Cooked Goose.

"What kind of mistakes?" I asked. As long as she was confessing, who was I to interfere?

"On this one I sewed the geese both backwards and upside-down." She seemed to let out a low moan.

"And this," she said, picking up a pile of sewn-together confetti. "This is where I used the wrong size needle and ripped the paper pattern to shreds." She began to look miserable.

"Why didn't you fix them?" I asked helpfully. She could fix anything, I thought.

"I was going to," she began, but then her voice changed and she said, "but they can't really be fixed."

"So they're rags?" I asked.

"No, I didn't want to throw them out. I just can't throw anything out. I was saving them…."

"Saving them?"

"Well, it's so difficult to throw them out. I thought I'd use the fabric in something else or cut them up into patches or squares and donate them to someone else for quilts or…." She trailed off again. That was becoming a habit with her.

"But you don't need to keep them, do you?"

"Not really."

"So why don't we just clean house," I offered. "Let's get rid of them." Wasn't I the practical husband?

"I've been wanting to. I just don't feel I can."

"You don't have the guts?" I prodded. I would be the strong one.

"Help me," she pleaded. "I can't face it alone."

"You won't back out?" I asked. I could see her body tighten, and a grim look appeared on her face.

"I'll try," she said courageously. "I'll really try."

And she tried. She went to get a large plastic trash bag while I emptied out the pile from that closet. I didn't let her look at them. I pushed the orphaned quilt beginnings into the bag. "Where else?" I asked. She pointed to the bedroom. I led her to the back of the bedroom closet. There in the dark corner was another pile of terminally ill miniature quilt tops. Why hadn't I noticed them before?

"Mistakes?" I asked. I picked one out.

"The colors don't work together. I didn't know anything about contrasting colors when I began. I was just learning...." She seemed to shrink in her apology.

I stuffed the "rags" into the bag. "Next?" I asked.

"The kitchen," she said meekly. Off to the kitchen we went. In the cupboard under the sink were some small embroidered quilt squares. I couldn't read the embroidery or make out any legible design. "I used the wrong thread and the wrong needles and the wrong tensions," she confessed. "I saved them anyway, in case we ran out of kitchen towels," she explained.

"Well, we could use them if we have a flood and use up all the others," I agreed. "Or we might use them to wipe up water if you put too much garbage in the disposal and the sink overflows." She gave me a look and I shut up. I stuffed the embroidery mistakes into the bag. I did hesitate a moment, for they would make good rags for washing the car.

The big black bag was getting heavy. "Any more?"

"A few," she said. And we were off. Under the sink in the bathroom, the cupboard under the bookcase in the living room, the coat closet by the front door—all had a small pile of rags. Oops, sorry. I should have written "mistakes."

And she was honest about what she had done: uneven triangles, unsquared squares, two-inch strips that began at one end at two inches and ended up at the other about half-an-inch wide. (She didn't want Olfa to know.)

"They were beginner's mistakes," I said to comfort her.

"This one was yesterday," she said, showing me a square with two of the nine patches going the wrong way.

"It happens," I said philosophically.

Finally, when the bag was full, she said we had them all. I tied off the bag. "Are you sure now?" I asked, feeling some sympathy for her, feeling empathy for the choice she had to make. She had come face to face with her quilting past and it loomed out at her like some dark monster.

"I'm sure," she said, her lips quivering.

"No turning back?"

"No. Go ahead, take them to the thrift shop. Go now, before I change my mind." She pointed me to the door. I looked at her one more time to be absolutely sure. She had her hand covering her eyes, her palm toward me, the back of her hand shielding her view. "I'm all right," she whispered. "Go."

That was a week ago. Since then she has been fine. Oh, every once in a while I catch her staring off into space or opening a closet where the mistakes had been hidden in storage. And occasionally as she quilts she lets out a long, forlorn sigh, but all in all she has been brave. And I am proud of her for letting go. Still, now I have to find a new supply of dusting rags. She's no longer a beginner, so I can't expect her to provide any more now, can I?

30. All the Months

No, no, not again," she said. She was sitting at the kitchen table drinking her fifth cup of herbal peppermint tea when she put her teacup down with a hard bang.

"Too much tea?" I asked. I sat opposite her. I was reading the morning paper; she was reading one of her many quilt magazines. It was probably an article on quilting.

"This always happens," she said. She reached for some napkins and wiped at the tea that had spilled from her cup.

I knew a lead-in line when I heard one, so I asked, "What always happens?" My first thought was the magazine contained a photo of a quilt so exquisite, so beautiful, that it was impossible for any normal quilter ever to attempt, let alone complete. She usually yelled or screamed at the teasing photo, but she had never before banged down her cup.

"These directions," she answered. She was calming down, but her voice still trembled.

"Bad directions?" I asked. She shook her head. "They call for too much fabric?" I asked. She had once shown me a design for a miniature quilt in a magazine that asked her to buy twelve rotary cutters, sixteen yards of batting, eighteen yards of fabric, fifty-four spools of thread, and a new house. Or so it seemed.

"They're good directions. They're clear directions," she told me.

"Put down your dander," I said. Her dander was still up and it was hard to see her through it. She calmed down a bit more.

"I am calm," she said.

"So it's a terrible design with good directions?" I asked. I was patient. My checklist of what could have gotten her so riled up was very short. That was the last question on my list.

"The design's simple and the directions are clear," she said.

"So what's wrong?" I asked. That was the bonus question.

"What's wrong? What's wrong? I'll tell you what's wrong." But she didn't tell me just yet. She began flipping through other pages of the magazine, reading a moment, staring at a photo a moment, then flipping some more pages. Then she pushed the magazine aside and did the same with two more in her pile. She did this quickly as I sat and stared at her, waiting for an explanation.

"December, October, March, June," she said.

"They're all good months," I said. Since we had both retired, all months were good.

"I don't have all the months," she said.

"How many are you missing?" I asked. I knew there were only twelve months. I also knew about seven days in a week. Sixty minutes in an hour.

"November and January and…." Her voice dropped then rose again. "Oh, it's no use. I'll probably need some years, too. I hate it." Her dander was back up.

"Have some more tea," I said.

"You want to know what I'm talking about, don't you?" she asked.

"I want to help you," I said. Since she had taken up quilting, I have tried to make our home a safe environment for her. I haven't padded the walls yet, but at that moment, the thought was circling my mind.

"There's nothing you can do," she said. She pushed the magazines away from her.

"Do you want to talk about it?" I asked. I piled the magazines together and pushed them across the table, far away from her. I took her hand.

"You'll think I'm getting upset over nothing," she said.

"If you get upset, it must be something important," I said. My quilting spouse is usually tough as nails, stronger than steel, more stable than Mt. Rushmore. But she is joined at the hip, the brain, and the charge card with thousands of quilters all over the world. If she gets upset, it must be something important.

"Hand me the magazine on top," she said.

"Are you sure?" She seemed calm again.

"I can handle it," she said.

I handed her the magazine. She flipped it open, turned several pages, read a moment, and then slid the magazine across the table to me, her fingers holding her place.

"Read that," she said. I read the paragraph of directions she pointed out to me. They were clear, though I had little idea what they had to do with anything.

"I read it," I said.

"Did you read it all?"

"I read it all," I said. But to be sure I read it again. "So?" I asked, truly puzzled. She reached over and pointed to a line between parentheses in the middle of the paragraph. I read it out loud.

"(For a complete illustration for putting these blocks together, refer to the July 1998 issue.)"

"There, you see?" she said. "You see what's making me crazy?"

I saw. "You don't have the July 1998 issue?"

"I never have any of the issues they refer to. They do it to drive me crazy. Even if I had that issue, it would refer me to March 1997 or May 1954 or July 2001."

"They want you to buy all the magazines?" I said.

"They begin an article and give directions and just as I begin to get excited about making whatever quilt it is, and they always show this gorgeous color photo of it, that's when they pull out the carpet from under my feet and say, 'continued next month.'"

"They pull out the carpet?" We haven't had carpets like that in our house in thirty years, I thought. Our wall-to-wall carpet is nailed to the flooring just so no one could pull it out from under us, but I got her message.

"So what do you want to do about it?" I asked. She could stop buying the quilting magazines, I foolishly thought.

"I'm going to subscribe to them all," she said. "I'm going to buy all the back-issues in the world. I'm going to every garage sale in the western United States."

"That's a lot of magazines," I said, but I didn't doubt her. I remembered not believing her when she said she would buy all one hundred fourteen colors of Kona cotton. Four days later the UPS man struggled under that burden.

"Yes, well, maybe not all of them."

"Just the July 1998 issue?" I asked with hope in my heart.

"To begin with," she said. "But if it refers me to another article...."

PART 8

CRANBERRY SAUCE X 100 =

MINIATURE QUILTS
FABRIC GOES FURTHER

31. Tell Me Why

She was sitting at her machine, the light over her head casting her shadow down on the lonely marine-blue cotton triangles she was turning into happy marine-blue squares. But she wasn't sewing. She was barely moving. I went into one of her desk drawers and pulled out a small mirror and held it up in front of her lips to see if she was breathing. She was, but barely.

"What is it?" I asked. This was not her normal position, frozen in place. She should have been humming along with her machine, turning out a dozen squares a minute, her body in spirited animation.

"I've been thinking," she answered quietly.

"Thinking about what?" I asked in my best investigative manner.

"Why I quilt," she said with a sigh.

"You've been sitting there in suspended animation wondering why you quilt?" I asked. "You know why you quilt. You quilt for fun, for excitement, for the pleasure of providing your loving husband with a quilt to keep him warm through icy winters."

"It's not always fun," she said. "And our winters aren't icy."

"What do you mean it's not always fun?" To me sixty-eight degrees in the house is icy.

"Well, it's not fun when my bobbin thread breaks eighty-seven times in a row or when I cut ten strips of fabric too small to use or I run the rotary cutter off the mat and slice the edge off my table."

"Well, those were adventures, learning experiences. You've never complained before." Oh, she was frustrated at times, as when she discovered that she was short one strip of odd blue fabric that was no longer in her stash or even in existence anywhere. Or when she sewed seven triangles together backwards. Or when she had discovered one of the blocks in her finished quilt was in the wrong place. But she had always expressed happiness before. "What about all the other reasons you quilt?"

"I've been thinking about that, how many reasons I really have for quilting." She seemed without emotion as she spoke. But her body moved slightly on her chair, and I did see her blink. She was definitely alive.

"How about ten reasons," I suggested. "Just try to come up with your top ten reasons for quilting. They have the top ten reasons for everything else on television. You can have them, too." I went to her desk and grabbed a pencil and a piece of paper. "I'll write them down for you," I said.

"But they may not be good reasons," she said. My wife the pessimist. She seemed a stranger to me.

"Don't be a pessimist," I said. "Give me one reason. We'll start with one reason."

"To avoid having to play the tuba," she said.

"What? You never played the tuba in your life. You're not taking this seriously, are you?"

"No, I just don't have any good reasons."

"How about pleasing your family?"

"I don't have to quilt to do that. I can just send everyone money to buy a quilt at some department store."

"It's not exactly the same. The quilt labels won't say, 'Made With Love by Grandma or Mom or Dear Wife.' They'll say, 'Made by a Stranger in a Really Far Away Place Like China by People Who Don't Even Know You.'"

"All right, but that's the only reason I quilt."

"Is it? Is it really?" I said, feigning an angry rage, puffing out my cheeks and bellowing my words. "What about quilting because it's relaxing? Because it's creative? Because it provides adventure? Because it keeps your brain from atrophying?" She smiled at that. "Because it makes you smile?" I went on. "Because it keeps you from going out on the streets late at night selling drugs or breaking into stores or stealing hubcaps?"

"I don't do any of those things," she said, more animated now.

"Only because you are safe in this house hiding behind your mountains of stash."

"So, what else, Mr. Know-It-All?" she asked. She even turned her head a few inches to look at me.

"So, what else is that you have the satisfaction of knowing how to use a rotary cutter, how to make a quarter-inch seam, and how to paper-piece a thousand birds in a forest. How many people do you meet who can do all that?"

She looked stunned at the thought. "What else?" she said, softening.

"Saving money," I said, though I knew that was not true. "We could buy out all the quilts in Quilts Is Us for what it cost you to make one twelve inch by twelve inch miniature wallhanging. I have three filing cabinets full of receipts just from quilting stores. UPS stock keeps rising because of you."

"Ha! There's no such store. Is there?"

"And you quilt because otherwise I would be too embarrassed to let anyone come into the bedroom and see some raggedy old comforter on the bed instead of your beautiful Amish quilt."

"We lived all these years without that quilt."

"Then how about the joy you felt when you learned to recognize and name a hundred fourteen colors of Kona cotton?"

"The names are on the color card that came with the fabric," she said, but it was a feeble protest.

"But you can distinguish between bright periwinkle and amethyst and iris and lilac." They all looked purple to me.

"Periwinkle is nice," she said.

"And remember how much fun you had after you learned how to make a Log Cabin square?"

"That was fun," she said.

"Even after you went berserk and made three hundred of them?"

"I had to practice," she replied seriously. "Why are you writing all this down?" she said as she watched me scribbling furiously.

"Just taking a few notes," I said.

"What for?"

"Because people who don't quilt always ask me why you quilt. I never was sure before."

"Do you know why I quilt now?" she said as she stood away from her machine, went to one of her stacks of fabric, pulled down a large piece of marbled yellow batik, and covered me in it. "I'll tell you why I'm going to quilt right this moment," she said as she pulled me toward the sewing machine. "And you can tell everybody the reason. You are a madman."

"Oomph, mmmmm, owwww," was all I could say.

32. Waste Not, Want Not

*I*t's your fault, you know," she said.

"How is it my fault?" I asked.

"You bought that book for me."

"I didn't say you had to buy six thousand yards of fabric," I said.

"I bought only six yards," she said.

"Six yards of this and six yards of that," I said.

"Stack-n-Whack takes a lot of fabric," she said.

She was just finishing up her first Stack-n-Whack quilt and the hook was already in and set. She was being pulled up into a boat that was taking her into unknown waters. But she was a willing catch. "I'm going to do a lot of these," she said as she looked up from the final stages of her first Kaleidoscope quilt.

"And you need all that fabric for each one?" She had been talking about cutting away from the selvage, cutting long strips, design repeat lengths, and a lot of other quilting gobbledygook. All right, jargon. All right, quilting terminology.

"More fabric than you would believe," she said.

"The book says so?"

"The book says so." Yes, I had given her the book as a Tuesday present several weeks before, but now I doubted how good an idea that had been. She had begun the new Stack-n-Whack quilt a week before as an experiment, an impossible dream, a quest for some golden quilt grail.

With fear of failure in her quilting head and trepidation shaking her quilting hands that day, she had scrounged through her pile of "Last Resort" fabric, flea market and ninety-percent-off sale fabric that she thought she would never have any possible use for. It was fabric that she would lose no sleep over if a gang of thieves broke in late at night and stole it. I think she had it because it cost only ten cents a yard.

She had begun expecting complete failure, a total mess, a frustrating voyage into quilting hell, but she had managed to put together a throw quilt. She had whacks and points and a backing and a border and a binding. She had a finished Stack-n-Whack quilt. And now she was over the edge. Though, like some Rumpelstiltskin changing flax into gold, she had turned "cheap" fabric into a "priceless" quilt, she now wanted to make another one, and she wanted first-class fabric, quality fabric, and in six-yard lengths.

"Miniature quilts," I said. "You have three books and four magazines devoted to miniature quilts." I tried to divert her back to reality and less fabric.

"What?" she asked, her full attention given to the sixteen tons of new expensive fabric she was unfolding.

"Here's a pattern for an Amish quilt that needs only a half-yard of fabric total," I said, pushing a magazine article toward her eyes.

"I'm busy here," she said, dismissing me.

"You're busy with enough fabric for a hundred miniature quilts or wallhangings or lap quilts or twin or full or queen- or king-sized quilts," I said.

"What?" she asked.

"Why do you need six yards of fabric for a quilt?" I asked. I knew it was a hopeless task to try to get her attention back when she was in quilting mode.

"The book says...."

"The book says you need six yards of fabric," I answered for her. "I know. But isn't there a smaller quilt in your book?"

"Of course," she said. She had both hands full of fabric, her arms encircling enough fabric for her to become another Christo and drape the Empire State Building. "But how much depends on the distance between the repeats," she said.

As I did not understand a word she said, I tried again. "Are you going to forgo all the other quilts you plan to make, the zillion projects you said you had to do in this and the next lifetime?"

"They can wait," she said.

"So you're going to make only Stack-n-Whack quilts from now on?" I asked. I tried to calculate what six yards per quilt for ten or twenty years of quilts would cost.

"I like this quilt," she said. She began to spread the fabric out flat on the table. "I like it so much I am going to make some more and more and more," she said. I knew she still wasn't paying attention to my great argument that she should make small quilts, quilts that would be less costly to the household budget.

"But—" I said. How could I reason with her? Then I remembered watching her cut the first strip of fabric for the very first "whack" of her quilt. "But you use only a small part of fabric when you cut it the way you have to for stacking it, even if it's eight layers high." I spoke as if I knew everything there was to know about what she was doing. "Some of the fabric is wasted," I added.

That caught her attention. "Waste? What waste? I do not waste fabric! The only wasted fabric in this house is the lint I clean out of the sewing machine or the dryer." I thought I saw her stomp her foot for emphasis, but maybe that was my imagination. Her words were emphatic enough. "And I'm still trying to think up a way to make a lint quilt," she added.

"But, but, all those pieces you cut off and you don't use—?" I sputtered.

"They're leftovers," she said.

"Like turkey leftovers you can eat later?" I asked.

"Exactly," she said.

"All right," I said. That sounded good to me. I can understand leftovers. "Waste not, want not," I said, but she was lost to me again. She had her ruler out and was measuring the designs on the fabric.

"Maybe I should have bought eight yards," she said.

It wasn't until today when she came into the house with more fabric that I learned that the six yards for the next quilt was only for the kaleidoscope blocks. Today I learned that she needed three yards or more for the background and almost half a yard or more for the accent, and three yards or more for the backing, and about a yard or more for the binding. I think I'll go lie down now.

33. The Low Cost of Quilting

How do you afford it?" our friends always ask.

"But doesn't all that fabric cost a fortune?"

"But don't all those quilting supplies cause bankruptcy?"

I always answer that we can't afford it, that fabric costs a fortune, and buying quilting supplies causes bankruptcy. Darling Wife the quilter, however, has a different answer for each question. All have to do with the fact that she has developed a quilter's brain, which is probably at an angle or pointed or squared off or stripped. No doubt her brain cells form a kaleidoscope or her brain is now pieced together following some pattern from a manual for beginner quilters.

"How much did that fabric cost?" I asked in her second month of quilting. She had just come back from some trip to some quilt shop where quilters talked to one another in secret code and encouraged each other as if they were all members of a 12-step quilting support group. All twelve steps, no doubt, had to do with spending more money at each step of the addiction that quilting brought to the innocent.

"Not much," she said.

"Not much how much?" I asked. Before she took up quilting, she would tell me how much she spent. Now, no doubt, after she had taken some quilters' vow of secrecy, she might evade, sidestep, mislead, or circumvent, but she would never lie.

"I got a great bargain," she said, sidestepping, misleading, evading, and circumventing.

"How much did the bargain cost?" I asked. The trick was to be persistent. Our retirement depended on it. We didn't have social security yet, and wiping windshields at stop signs didn't exactly appeal to me as a future job.

"Less than I thought," she said.

"How much less?" My tone of voice was designed to show my impatience with her answers.

"Do you want to know exactly?" She recognized the tone.

"How much did the fabric cost?" I asked.

"Twelve ice cream cones," she said.

That was eleven months ago and the beginning of her version of quilter accounting. Quilter accounting, according to my Dear Wife's new way of thinking, was designed to show that through careful budgeting, all her quilting was essentially cost-free. In fact, she was going to prove over the next quilt-filled shopping months, it would save money.

"Ice cream cones?" I asked her that day. "Twelve ice cream cones?"

"I'm not going to eat twelve ice cream cones," she said.

"And?" I asked her that day.

"Substitution," she said. "The money I save from not eating the ice cream cones will pay for the fabric." She was delighted with her version of new math, quilters' math.

"You're not going to eat twelve ice cream cones?" I asked, but I didn't expect any further explanation. She fooled me.

"Remember when you bought the computer four years ago?" she said.

"Yes," I said cautiously.

"And remember what you told people when they asked how you could afford such a nice computer?"

"Go on," I said.

"You told everybody that you didn't buy the more expensive car you wanted but settled for a less expensive one and used the difference to buy the computer."

"I said that?" I did say that. It made sense to me at the time.

"I'm not going to eat twelve ice cream cones, so I can buy the fabric with the money I don't spend."

"That makes sense," I said.

"And I have four dollars a day to spend because I don't smoke two packs of cigarettes."

"You haven't smoked in forty years."

"So, I bought the sewing machine with that money."

"I thought we bought the sewing machine with the money from the trip we didn't take to Fiji."

"We used that money for the trip to Paducah to see the Quilt Museum."

"I thought we paid for that trip by not eating caviar for breakfast each day."

"You don't like caviar," she said.

"I like turkey," I said.

"Yes, and I was able to buy all that batting by not buying a hundred cans of cranberry sauce."

"And we didn't have yams this year," I said.

"You don't eat yams. I bought bias tape with that money."

"And what else that I don't eat didn't you buy?"

"You're allergic to shrimp, so that paid for the quilt templates."

"How much shrimp didn't I eat?"

"About ten cans. I could have not bought fresh shrimp and saved even more money."

"I don't eat squid. I suppose you didn't buy any?"

"I didn't think of that. I do need some more black thread for the next quilt. I think not buying squid would take care of that."

"I seem to be making all the sacrifices."

"I gave up having my nails done."

"For what? You've never paid to have your nails done in your life."

"And I don't plan to in the future. I used that money to buy the three rotary cutters and the three Olfa mats."

And so it went and so it goes. Whenever I show her evidence of our going broke, she begins to sacrifice new things. This morning she was looking through the catalogs to find some new fabric for sashing the quilt she's working on. Halfway through the second catalog, she looked up at me as I crossed the room. "What?" I asked.

"Let's not climb Mount Everest for New Year's Eve," she said.

"I don't plan to go anywhere," I said.

"Good, then I can get the new quilt book, too."

"As long as it doesn't cost us anything," I said. And with her doing the accounting, we will probably make money on the purchase.

34. Bind for Glory

No, no, no," she yelled at the book she was reading. She was standing over the large ironing board in her sewing room, the book on one side and the strips of binding she was making for the new quilt on the other.

"You can't take that away from me," I finished, but from her tone and the frown on her face, I knew she wasn't singing some old song. She was upset and frustrated. "You upset?" I asked.

"I did the binding wrong," she said.

"How wrong?" I asked. I had become used to her saying she had done something wrong in her efforts to complete five hundred quilts in ten days, or so it seemed. I hadn't seen her much lately. She came out of her sewing room only on rare occasions, and mostly that was to exclaim that another quilt was finished. And she was never satisfied. Something was always wrong, she complained. A crooked square, a wavy sashing (I told her to wave back), a border that was off by a thousandth of an inch, a six-pointed star that had only five-and-a-half points. "Looks good to me," I always said.

"I followed the new instructions in this book," she said, holding a strip of blue fabric up to my face. "Just look at how this binding looks."

I looked at a blue blur as she passed it quickly in front of my eyes. "Looks fine to me," I said. I wasn't just being nice. It was a fine blur.

"I know it's fine. It's almost perfect, but it's not what the book says it should look like."

"Get another book," I said. And, that, of course, was the real problem. She had too many quilting books.

"But this is the new one I got for my birthday," she said, dropping the strip of fabric and lifting the book up to my face. *Four Billion and Eight Ways to Create the Perfect Binding*, the book title read.

"So, which one did you use?" I asked.

"I did Binding Number Forty-three. It says to cut the fabric on the bias and turn it toward the sunny side of the house and iron it with a cold iron while stretching it to the left," she said.

"Did you stand on one foot?" I asked. Sometimes quilting directions are a bit odd. But she always told me the Quilter's Creed was "Anything that works."

"Don't be silly," she said.

"I'm silly?" I asked. "I didn't turn the fabric to the sunny side of the house during the foggiest day of the year."

"You know I'm making that up. The instructions are clear and useful and easy to follow."

"So why are you yelling, 'No, no, no,' and frowning?" I asked.

"Because the book doesn't agree with my other books," she said, and she dropped the large book on the ironing board, right on top of the blue binding.

"So it's a book war?" I asked.

"It's a directions war," she said.

"You're having problems with the directions again?" I knew she had screamed early in her quilting life when she had followed the directions to cut out fabric to make a quilt, only to find out after all the fabric was cut out that the measurements in the book or magazine were wrong. After the second time she had done that she had learned to make only one square before she built the largest scrap heap in Quiltland from wrongly cut or wrongly sewn or wrongly batted or wrongly quilted fabric.

"I'm having trouble because I learned how to make binding a good way, and then I read directions for a new better technique for making binding, and then I read directions for a superior way to make binding, and then I read an article on eight hundred ways to avoid making bad binding, and then I read another article in a quilting magazine on how to make simple binding in an easy way, and the binding holding my head together is getting frayed." She said that all in one breath. Quilters can do that.

"Why don't you just go with what works," I suggested helpfully.

"They all work," she said, "but then an article in the latest issue of *Quilting Made Darn Easy* or the newest book, called *Cooking, Cleaning, and Making Binding in Your Spare Time*, comes along, and all the books say there's a new miracle technique for me to bind my way into heaven."

"How many quilts have you made so far?" I asked.

"A couple," she said, underestimating the truth by about a dozen, maybe two dozen. Lately, she's become a quilt factory.

"And they all have binding?"

"Of course."

"And you did the binding?"

"Who else lives in this house who has a terminal addiction to stash and stitches?" she asked.

"And all the bindings fit the quilts you made?"

"Yes," she said, looking at me now, her attention undivided, which was rare, as ninety percent of her attention the past year was always on some aspect of quilting.

"And you've made mock binding, and straight binding and bias binding with mitered corners and diagonal seams and French kisses…?"

"That's French binding," she said. She was paying attention.

"And lapped binding and single-fold and double-fold and scalloped…?"

"Do you know what you're talking about?" she asked.

"No, but sometimes you read out loud, and I pick up things."

"How about picking up the telephone and ordering me some more fabric so I can make more binding," she said. It wasn't a question. It wasn't a request. It was a quilter's command.

"What kind of binding?" I asked.

"I don't know yet. I'll see what the new book says."

"New book?"

"The one you're going to order for me."

"What book am I ordering for you?"

"*Dream Binding and Butter Churning Your Way into the New Year*," she said.

Why not?

PART 9

35. Rip Tide

Look at this," she said as she pushed the quilting book over toward me. I pushed aside my cup of coffee and, once again, looked at a page of quilts as she pushed the book under my nose.

"Very nice," I said, and I pushed the book back. I needed my coffee.

"You didn't even look," she said.

"I looked. It was a page of quilting designs." It was not too hard to guess that. All the pages of all the books she pushed under my nose had quilting designs on them. My life was one big quilting design.

"Not the designs," she said. "The quilting on the top quilt." She pushed the book back. I sipped my coffee, put the cup down, wiped my lips with a napkin, and looked at the page of quilting designs. The top one was a picture of a miniature quilt, blue six-pointed stars on a background of white.

"Nice quilt," I said. I pushed the book back.

"Look at the stippling," she said. She pushed the book back one more time.

"Nice stippling," I said.

"It's blue," she said.

"It's blue," I agreed. I really needed that coffee.

"It makes the stippling stand out. I'm going to try that," she said.

"Uhmm," I said. I was already sipping the coffee as she pulled the book back.

That was yesterday morning. By ten o'clock she had begun quilting the beautiful table runner she had completed the day before. By ten-thirty she had stippled the center squares of several stars. The stippling was blue. Blue against white. Blue on white. Blue!

"What do you think?" she asked as I stood at the bookcases looking for a book I had misplaced. We were in the living room. It used to be a living room. Now the furniture was all pulled back and three six-foot banquet tables filled the room. She sat at her sewing machine, the table runner spread out before her. One third of the runner had been stippled blue.

There is a time in every man's life when he must stand up for truth and justice and the American way. Yesterday morning was not one of those times. "Uhmmmm," I said, hoping I would get away with evasion. Ever since I had become a QS (Quilter's Spouse), I had learned there is a time and place to be silent.

"I didn't think so," she said.

"You didn't think what?" I asked. I hadn't said anything incriminating me.

"You don't like the stippling," she said.

"It's very nice stippling," I said. It was. But it was blue and took away from the design of the runner.

"But?"

"Uhmmmm," I said.

"It's too blue," she said. "I know. It takes away from the design of the runner."

"It's a little blue," I said.

"It looks worse every minute," she said.

"Uhm," I said, my grunt abbreviated.

"Maybe I should start all over," she said.

"Make a new quilt?"

"Yes."

"That's a lot of work," I said. I had watched her working on it for days. "Can't you just redo the stippling?" Now, to me, that was a logical suggestion. All she had to do was remove the stippling she had already done and redo it with white thread. Right?

"That's impossible," she said.

Sometimes it's foolish to ask the following question to a committed quilter, but foolishly I asked, "Why?"

"Tiny stitches. Millions of tiny stitches," she answered in a tone that suggested that any husband of a quilter should know that.

"I know that," I said. "But isn't it easier to take them out than start a new quilt?"

"Billions of tiny stitches through the quilt top and batting and backing," she said. She lifted up the runner and showed me a six-inch square of stippling. I saw billions of tiny stitches.

"Oh," I said.

"You want to rip them out?" she challenged.

"I don't quilt," I said. I silently moved my feet, turning them toward escape.

"Go ahead, try," she said.

"Do you have a seam ripper?" I asked.

"Hah!" she said.

"What's 'Hah'?"

"Too big. There are no seams."

"Well," I began, but I didn't finish my thought. I had no thoughts.

"Why are some of the stitches so close together?" I asked.

"Free-motion," she answered.

"Free what?" All I knew was "Free Willy."

"I can't always control the stitch size. The feed dogs are down."

"Oh, that explains it," I said. I don't understand quantum physics either.

I looked around her table and saw a tiny pair of embroidery scissors. I lifted up a section of the runner, turned it over, and picked at one of the stitches. She stood by my side silently, but I knew she was laughing out loud. Two minutes later, I had cut out a stitch. I caught my breath, and began a second stitch. That took only a minute. I took another deep breath and began the third. "A billion stitches?" I asked. She nodded.

It took me two hours, well past the time for lunch, but I removed the stitches from about five squares. She had joined me and had done about ten. Of course, she had chosen to do the long stitches, about a very easy free-motion inch apart, and I had to do the short stitches, something like eight hundred stitches to the inch. My back was broken from bending over the table. My eyes would never see anything close up again. I lost eight or ten pounds. My fingers were gnarled and stiff. A quilt of shredded stitches covered my clothes, my face, and every bit of my body.

"You're a good ripper," she said as I pulled the last blue thread through the quilt sandwich.

"Ripper?" I thought I was a quilter. I earned being called a quilter. I wanted a badge, a trophy, and some recognition.

"You should have told me the blue wouldn't look good when I showed you the picture in the book."

"Would that have stopped you?"

"No. It looked like a good idea."

"So what are you going to do now?" I asked as I hobbled over to the sofa and collapsed.

"I'm going to stipple," she said.

"In white?"

"What else?" she said.

I kept my mouth shut.

I am now revising my monthly list of survival resolutions. I am adding one that has something to do with stitches and stippling and ripping and ripping and ripping.

36. A Quilter's Day Off

I'm taking the day off," she said. She had just finished the new quilt for our grandson's next birthday, and now she felt she needed some rest.

"What day are you taking off?" I asked. She had before promised to take a day off, but unless I yanked her out of the house, into the car, and to some isolated spot in some wilderness with nary a quilt shop in sight, she wouldn't have taken a day off all year.

"Sunday. Sunday will be my day of rest," she said.

"Sounds like a good day," I said. That was on Saturday.

On Sunday morning, she was up long before dawn, as usual, and I found her in the kitchen. The counter was covered with boxes and bowls and the supplies to feed most of the western half of the United States. "It's cold and drizzly out," she said. "I'm going to cook today."

"I thought today was your day off."

"It's my day off from quilting," she said. "Cooking relaxes me."

"I thought quilting relaxed you."

"It does. But I'm not quilting today. I'm relaxing by cooking and freezing enough food for the rest of the century."

"All right," I said, agreeable to a fault.

That was at four AM. At five AM I heard her in her sewing room. I got up from my desk where I had been looking over the totals of her spending on quilting fabrics and supplies for the year so far. Just as I was about to look at the final total and file for bankruptcy, I heard her closet door open and close and open again. I went to see what the commotion was all about.

"What is all the commotion about?" I asked. "I thought you were in the kitchen cooking."

"I am, but I just remembered something I needed to do before I put the enchiladas in the microwave."

"Something to do with your cooking?" I asked. On her ironing board was a microwave dish full of enchiladas.

"I was pouring the enchilada sauce on the enchiladas when I remembered some fabric I put away last summer."

"And you came in here with your enchiladas?"

"I'm putting them in to microwave in a minute. But I couldn't remember where the fabric was. It has a western theme and I thought I'd use it for a wallhanging for the kids." The kids were our thirty-four-year-old son and his wife, who had just decorated their new house using a southwestern theme.

"Did you find it?" Of course, she did. She was holding the folded fabric in her hands.

"I just wanted to find it. Now I'm going to go back to my cooking," she said. With that, she put the fabric on her ironing board and picked up the microwave dish with her enchiladas. I followed her out of the room back to the kitchen. She went back to cooking.

A half-hour later she was rummaging in the hall closet. "Are you looking for the turkey?" I asked.

"The turkey's in the kitchen," she said. "I was just looking for the new batting we put away. I can't find it."

"Batting? What about the turkey?"

"I was looking for the baster, and that made me think about batter for the muffins, and that made me think about the batting."

"All Bs?" I guessed.

"What?"

"Never mind. The batting's in the cupboard in the garage. You told me to put it there when it came last month."

"Oh, good, now I can roast the turkey."

Forty-five minutes later she was standing at the kitchen counter opening brass safety pins. I didn't say a word. I just stood watching her until she realized I was there. That took about five minutes.

"I'm waiting for the yogurt to cool down," she said. "I thought I'd open all the new quilting pins so they'd be ready for the next time I basted a quilt." Of course, no better time than the present.

By lunch time she had strayed several more times. She had been opening a can of olives when she remembered the disarray in her quilting drawer, that drawer left a mess when she had finished the last quilt. She spent the twelve minutes the muffins were in the oven (on the rack below the turkey) sorting her notions. Then while she was putting the last batch of soiled utensils into the dishwasher, she had gone into the cutting room off the kitchen to put a new blade into her rotary cutter. She saved the old blade in case she had to cut through paper. During the morning she had also managed to pin together the pieces for some blocks, sorted her Kona cotton into "color families," and tested some unknown fabric she found while looking for a four-quart stock pot in the garage cupboard by burning a piece of the fabric to see if it was cotton. It melted into a glob of polyester. Finally, she cut out and quilted new oven mitts to take out the turkey safely. "It's not real quilting," she explained. "We need them."

After lunch, during which she read through two new quilting magazines, marking their pages with Post-It Note tabs so she could get to "those neat projects" sometime in the future, she said, "It's so nice to have a whole day off from quilting." Then she went into her sewing room "just for a second" to put away the magazines. When she didn't come back right away, and the timer on the oven beeped for the turkey, I went to look for her. She sat at her sewing machine pushing her right hand down and lifting it back up.

"What now?" I asked. She held up her hand to me. She held one of her many pincushions. "Yes?" I asked, seeing lots of glass-headed quilting pins. But then I looked closer. I didn't see any pins. I only saw their blue and yellow heads.

"The grandchildren," she said.

"Go on," I prompted.

"I told them not touch anything in here…."

"They touched something?" I asked. What grandkids wouldn't? A sewing room was a paradise for their curiosity.

"They pushed in all the pins on all the pincushions. I have to pull them all out."

"Now?" Of course, now. "The turkey's done," I said.

"You get it," she said. "I'll be right in."

I got the turkey. I took it out of the oven, my hands protected by newly quilted oven mitts. I took the turkey out of the pan and I began taking it apart. I waited for her to come to my side to finish up, but I waited in vain. I stripped the turkey, cleaned up the mess, disposed of the carcass, and went to look for her.

"Honey," I said as I went into the sewing room, but she was not there. I looked under the sewing table, in the closet, in each of the twenty-four drawers of fabric, in the closet again, and finally deduced that she was not there. I went on a room-to-room search. I found her in the living room pulling quilting books off of her shelf.

"They're out of order," she said. "I'm just putting them back in order so I'll be able to find the information when I need it."

"O.K. Sure," I said.

"When I'm done here, I'm just going to relax some more," she said.

"You look relaxed now," I said.

"I am. I'm glad I decided to take today off from quilting."

"Me, too," I said.

37. Quiltouflage

"Come in here," she commanded. Obediently, I put down the book I was reading and rushed down the hall to her sewing room.

"What?" I asked, wondering if some catastrophe had visited the room or whether she had a new quilt finished for me to look at. The way she had yelled, it could have been either one.

She didn't answer, but she pointed at the new design wall I had put up two days before. Previously, the design wall had been an old flannel white sheet that rippled and billowed from the slightest breeze, let alone the overhead fan that she turned on when the room got too hot, probably from overheating the sewing machine as she quilted endlessly. Now it was a smooth wall of flannel, the backing of vinyl tablecloth material cut to fit and stapled tight to the wall. On that smooth surface hung her newly assembled wallhanging top. A garden scene of rabbits and flowers and bees and leaves hung on the wall in happy profusion.

"Very nice," I said, and I turned to leave, to get back to my book.

"Not so fast. Look again." Knowing her tone of voice had changed to one which said, "Look or suffer a terrible fate," I looked again.

"It's still very nice," I said.

"It's crooked," she said. "It's bent. It's flawed."

"You want me to look at it and tell you it's not perfect?" Did she want me to end our marriage right then?

"I thought it looked good, but then you looked at it and said it was tilted."

"I didn't say a word," I protested. Would I jump into traffic from an overpass during rush hour? I knew better.

"You looked at it," she said. "You looked at it, and every part of your body said it was helter-skelter."

"It's not helter-skelter," I said.

"Look at it again," she said. "Honestly."

I looked at it again. "I'm looking honestly," I said. Two of the blocks were very slightly off. The top of one block was very, very slightly, tilted up. "It's a tiny, tiny bit skewed up." I said.

"What did you say?" she asked, alarmed in some quilter's way.

"I said it was a tad oblique."

"All right," she said.

"But it's very nice," I said.

"Oblique means slanted. That means it's crooked," she said.

"Can I go now?" I asked softly. I wanted to go. I didn't want to face her trip to the depths of quilter's depression.

"I can fix it," she said.

I recovered my breath and was about to ask her again if I could leave, but she was no longer aware that I was in the room. She was pulling down the wallhanging. I disappeared.

Several hours later, when I was in the kitchen preparing my lunch, not knowing when I would ever see her again, I heard her voice shake the house again. "Come in here," she said.

I put down the bread, I put away the sliced turkey, I put away the mustard, and I went. I went very cautiously to the back of the house and her sewing room.

"What?" I asked.

She didn't answer. She pointed to the design wall where her wallhanging hung.

"Very nice," I said. I was cautious and careful and cowardly.

"Look at it," she said. "It's fixed."

"Fixed?" I looked with my eyes open this time. What was hanging before me was the same wallhanging, but I didn't see any mistakes, any crookedness, any helter-skelter, any oblique or skewed anything. I was astonished. Everything looked perfect. I couldn't believe it was the same wallhanging. Maybe she had made a new one.

Stories by Popser

"It's the same one," she said, absolutely knowing what I was thinking at every moment.

"It looks… perfect," I said. I hoped that was the right thing to say.

"Ask me why it looks good now," she said.

"Why does it look good now?" I asked.

"Quiltouflage," she said.

"What kind of flage?" I asked, pronouncing it "flahge." Will I ever learn all those quilting terms?

"I covered up all the mistakes so no one can see them. Like camouflage. You don't see any mistakes, do you?" She meant, "You had better not see one stitch out of place."

"I don't see any mistakes," I said. I did notice some additions.

"I added yo-yos and buttons and more flowers and more leaves and more appliqué and fancy stitches and a few other things. Then I added some quilting all over the cricks and cracks."

"I don't remember any cricks and cracks," I said.

"They're gone. I stippled over everything to cover all the mistakes," she said happily.

"So you're covering the slight variations that were previously obvious in the wallhanging by making them appear to be part of their natural surroundings?" I asked. "In other words, concealment by disguise?"

"Huh?"

"Quiltouflage," I said.

"Absolutely. With quiltouflage, even you, Mr. Smarty-pants, can't tell."

"I can tell when it's time to go have lunch," I said.

"Make me a turkey sandwich," she said. "All this quilting makes me hungry."

I began thinking about disguising the turkey with mustard and lettuce and tomatoes and pickle. What would that be called?

38. Toppers

When I walked into her sewing room to ask her about going for a walk, she was finishing up the binding on the largest quilt she had ever made, the quilt spread out over her flat-top ironing board and over the sides and down onto most of the floor. She was hand-stitching the binding to the quilt, and as the needle did its work, she kept muttering, "Never again. I'm not doing this again. Never again."

"Do you plan to give up quilting?" I asked.

"Never," she said.

"But you just said...."

"I just said I will never again make a quilt larger than a postage stamp."

"That's very small," I said. I tried to image the size of the triangles and squares and batting and sashing and binding that would go into that small a quilt.

"I'm just using hyperbole," she said. "The way you do all the time."

"I don't go beyond the truth," I said. Well, maybe a little.

"No more queen-size quilts. No more doubles. I'm sticking to twins, lap-size, crib-size, wallhangings, little quilts, and miniatures."

"You don't like queen-size any more?" I asked. I wanted to be sure of what she was saying. With quilters, well, you never really know when they'll change their minds.

"Too much fabric, too much batting, too much backing, too much expense, too much time, too much everything."

"You told me you liked making this quilt."

"I did. I liked making the top. I can handle the top. But putting the quilt together on the sewing machine and then rolling the quilt and shoving it back and forth and all around through the machine for days until it's all quilted, that's a lot of work."

"You never complained before," I said.

"I'm not complaining. I'm just swearing off really big quilts. I'm getting the monkey off my back. I'm going cold turkey. I'm going into rehab. I'm signing up to go to the Betty Ford Clinic for Big Quilters."

"You're not a big quilter," I said. She was four foot eleven inches and weighed about a pound, maybe two.

"I'm talking about the size of the quilts," she said.

"But you said you like the tops," I said.

"Lots of quilters like the tops. They just don't like the middles and the bottoms."

"So just make tops."

"I'm not a topper," she said.

"Oh," I said. What in heck was she saying now? I didn't have a quilter's secret decoding ring, so I waited for her to explain.

"Some people are toppers," she said. "Lots of people are toppers."

"Is that a real word?" I asked. I ask that every time she opens her mouth about quilting. One never knows with these people.

"It is now."

"They're people who only like making the tops," I guessed. I am a great guesser when it comes to her vocabulary. I am usually wrong, but every once in a while I come close.

"I was just reading about quilters who had a survey about how many unquilted tops they had."

"You have a couple," I said.

"They're just not finished yet. I plan to finish them."

"That's good," I said.

"One woman in the survey said she had thirty-three."

"That's a lot of quilts," I said.

"Not quilts, tops."

"Oh," I said.

"Some people love making tops. Then they have someone else quilt them."

"Does that count?"

"Of course that counts. Some people only do the quilting."

"Then they're not toppers?" I didn't want to guess what word she would come up with for them.

"I heard that some people only make the blocks, the squares. They don't even make tops."

"Wow!" I said.

"Now you're making fun," she said, her tone of voice getting a bit cool, berating me.

"I didn't know that. I thought everyone made whole quilts."

"Some people don't even do borders," she said rather matter-of-factly.

"They stop before the borders?" I was getting deeper and deeper into territory I should have known to stay out of.

"They like the designing, the assembly, the sewing, but then they stop short of the border."

That was too tempting. "They need passports to cross the border?"

"You're going to need a passport to keep on living," she said.

"I'm only trying to understand what you're saying," I said.

"I'm saying that some quilters like to quilt whole quilts and some just like to make the tops and some people just do the final quilting."

"I'm still thinking about quilts without borders," I said.

"I'm thinking about finishing this Godzilla-sized quilt and making something small." She turned the quilt and began stitching the last corner. Her fingers held the needle firmly and it disappeared in a blur of motion.

"Your next quilt will have a small top and a small middle and a small bottom?"

"I'm going to make you smaller," she said.

"I'm not a quilt," I said.

"You very well could be," she said, picking up her scissors, cutting off the last piece of thread, and wielding the very sharp blades in front of me.

I backed up, turned, and got my top and bottom out of there.

39. Visitors Day

She didn't pack her bags or get ready as she would for a regular trip, but she prepared herself nevertheless. She didn't pack a lunch or take a thermos of water as she would on a trip out of town. But she got herself ready nevertheless.

She put away the box of quilting equipment she kept at her side as she quilted. She turned off the sewing machines and covered them. She took down the last scrap of color from her design wall. She closed all her quilting books and magazines and put them on the shelves where they belonged. Then she took a long, deep breath, smiled, and began.

"You're not quilting today?" I had asked her earlier that morning as I saw her begin the preparations.

"Not today," she said.

"Are you feeling all right? A little tired? Upset stomach? Headache?" Something had to be wrong.

"I feel great, but I can't quilt today."

"You're planning to go shopping for more fabric?" I asked. That was as good a guess as I could make. I never could be sure of what this Darling Wife, a quilter, might be up to if she weren't quilting.

"I'm staying in the house all day. It's time."

"It's time?" I asked. Did it involve me? Was she going to yank me out of my daily laziness? I didn't want to get involved in any of her plans that day. I had plans of my own that didn't involve anything more than sitting or reclining or lying as flat as I could as I wasted away the day.

"It's visitors day," she said.

"Oh," I said, wondering at just that moment who was sick and why she hadn't told me about it. She didn't know anyone at any prison in the United States, so I didn't think that was it.

But she knew what I might be thinking. She always did. "It's the stash," she said.

"The stash is sick?" I asked. No, of course not. It couldn't be anything like that.

"It's been a while," she said.

"It's been a while," I repeated as any quilting husband would. I would repeat anything she said until I got it right and understood it. Sometimes that took all day.

"You know what I mean," she said.

"I do?"

"I just told you."

"You did?"

"The stash. I have to visit my stash. Today is the day I've set aside to do that."

At that moment I took everything she said, arranged it in my mind, rearranged it, and it still didn't make much sense to me. "You have to visit your stash," I said, taking the chance that I had heard her correctly.

"Most of the stash is lonely," she said. I just looked at her. "I've been so busy quilting lately, concentrating on what I was doing, playing favorites…." She looked at me as if to see if I was going where she was going. I wasn't. "I neglected most of the stash," she explained.

"Aha!" I said. I could have said, "Eureka!" or "Wow!" or I could have had a bright light bulb appear over my head. But I still didn't know down what path this Darling Wife of mine was traveling. "Go on," I said.

"Follow me," she said.

As always, when given the chance, I followed. She led me two feet away to the first set of her plastic drawers, which was part of her Fort Knox of stored stash. All in all she had twenty-one such drawers in three stacks of seven each against one wall of her sewing room. She pulled a drawer out of the frame that held it. "I see yellow fabric," I said. It was exactly what I saw. A plastic drawer full of yellow fabric.

"There are seven tones of solid yellow," she said. "The next drawer has the yellow prints, and under that there are the yellow reproduction designs. I haven't used yellow lately. So all this fabric has been left alone, dark inside these drawers, lonely and worried, neglected for weeks."

"So you're saying hello to all the yellow fabric?" I asked.

"I'm visiting it. I'm looking at it and taking it out and handling it and letting it know that I know it's there."

"You're visiting the fabric?" How dumb could I be? Not just a simple hello, but a real visit. Did she plan tea with it?

"I have to visit all the fabric today. All of these…." She swept out her arm to let me know she had twenty-one drawers of fabric to visit.

"That shouldn't take long," I said, hoping that it wouldn't take too long and that maybe we could go for a ride to the park and feed the ducks our leftover bread, which had been waiting for a visit to the ducks. I understand visiting ducks.

"I have to visit *all* the stash," she said again, emphasizing the word "all."

"All over the house?" The ducks might starve by the time that was over.

"Some I haven't seen for months," she said. "It needs to be taken out so I can remember where it is, what I have, and how much there is. I forget what I have sometimes, so I have to visit all the stash. I keep finding fabric I've forgotten about completely. If I didn't visit, it might get lost forever."

"Are you going to talk to it?" I asked, knowing that she often talked to her stash. Every scrap, every fat eighth or fat quarter, every half yard, every yard, every bolt of fabric she ever knew, she talked to it all.

"I'm just going to visit and say hello."

"And have tea?" She gave me a look that warned of danger.

"You visit all your books once in a while. You always tell me you found a book on the shelf that you had forgotten you had."

She had me there. "I have to dust the books occasionally," I tried. She didn't have to dust her fabric. All of it was bagged, boxed, wrapped, and safe in drawers or on shelves.

"I have to go now," she said, dismissing my answer and me. She had that intent look on her face now that meant that I had better flee to safety before she turned me into stash.

"When will you be back?" I asked.

"When visitors day is over," she said.

I went to visit my books. I wasn't going to say hello or talk to them.

But I thought about bringing coffee.

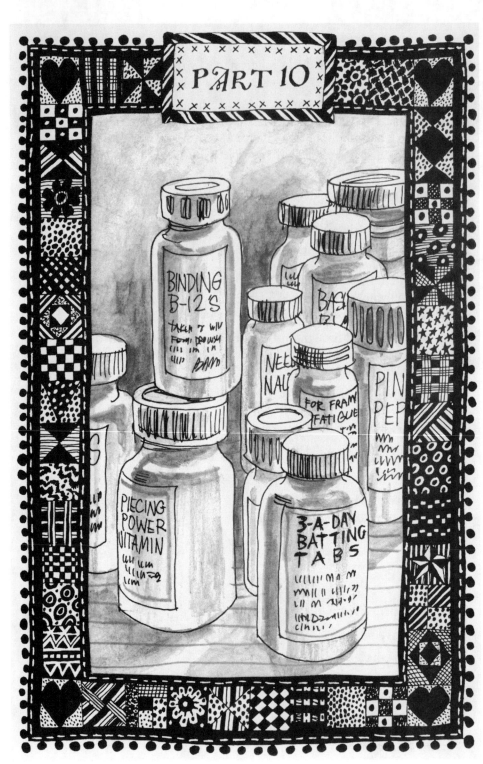

PART 10

40. Blue Moon

*I*t was this past Tuesday, the second day of the month, a rare month that would have two full moons, and I was cleaning out the flower beds and was making my way to the bed of yellow pansies I had planted in a window box. As I got closer, I was astonished to see the yellow pansies had bloomed again; only this time, the flowers were a pretty blue, rather than their natural color of yellow. I was so amazed I went back into the house, washed my hands free of soil and debris, and went to my Darling Wife's sewing room to bring her outside to witness this botanical miracle.

Reluctantly, she stopped and put down the rotary cutter she was holding over some blue fabric that was destined to be sewn into a new quilt, and she looked up to me as I beckoned her out of the room. "This had better be good," she said. It had to be some enormous event to drag her away from her quilting.

"Just wait," I said as I pulled her through the hallway, past the kitchen, and outside the house. I pointed at the planter box outside the kitchen window. "The pansies are looking great," I said proudly.

She looked. "The flowers are all blue," she said. "That's impossible. What did you do to them?" She looked away from the planter box and straight at me.

"I didn't do anything. It has to be a miracle."

"Did you use Miracle-Gro?" she asked.

"No. I haven't fertilized them yet."

"What happened to the old yellow-colored pansies?"

"They were yellow when I watered yesterday."

"And now we have blue pansies?" She was very dubious.

"Beauty is in the eye of the beholder," I said wisely.

"I'll decide that," she said. She turned from me and moved closer to the planter box. "They look blue," she said. "But they don't smell blue."

"How does blue smell?" I asked. I didn't know colors smelled. Of course, she did have a sixth sense about color. Hadn't she once told me she could smell the aroma of fabric colors? I didn't really believe her. Did I?

"Blue smells like blue. Pale blue smells like pale blue. Sky blue smells like sky blue. Navy blue smells like navy blue."

"I didn't know you could distinguish the shades." I was very skeptical.

"Anyway," she said, "they don't smell blue." She moved closer to the plant and began to lean toward it. She reached out her hand to a blossom. She took it in her hand. She sniffed it. Then she stood, petals in hand.

"So?" I asked. Now did she believe me?

She didn't answer right away. She looked around the planter box. She looked above the planter box. My eyes followed hers. I saw what she saw. There was the wall of the house, the kitchen window, and the spider web that stretched from under the eaves two feet across to the dryer vent. I saw a large spider prowling the web, looking for a meal. "Hah!" she said as she turned back to me.

"Hah?" I didn't see anything to "Hah" at. Then she began to laugh. And she laughed. And laughed.

"So, you've become hysterical over a miracle of nature?" I asked. She had something up her sleeve. I knew she did.

"Blue pansies," she laughed. She laughed at me. Me, her darling husband! She stopped laughing a moment, chuckled, and held out her hand with the blue blossom she had picked. "Look," she said.

I looked as she pushed her hand closer and closer to my face, right up to my eyes. I focused. I looked hard.

"Thread bunnies," she said.

"What?"

"You know what dust bunnies are?"

"Dust motes," I answered wisely.

"These are blue motes. Or in your case, thread and lint blossoms."
She grinned. Oh, it seemed a very evil grin.

"What are you saying?" Somehow she had gone from nature back to
quilting.

"The petals are all the color of the fabric I bought yesterday, aren't
they?" Her smile curled.

I did remember her bringing home more fabric. Was it blue? I wasn't
sure. I looked at what I had in my hand. My blossom was a small ball
of tangled blue thread. Periwinkle blue, I decided. "Your fabric was
periwinkle blue," I said smartly.

"I washed the fabric and it must have unraveled along the selvage and
some threads came loose and the dryer spit the blue threads and blue
lint out of the vent right above the planter box." For some reason she
laughed again.

I looked up at the vent. I looked down at the plant. I reached for the
blossoms. One after another. They were all little tangled messes of
thread and lint. "Thread and lint bunnies," I said, now all-knowing.
But I could catch her yet. "So why can't you smell their color?"

"They're dried flowers," she said. "They've lost their fragrance."

"Oh," I said.

"And your job is to pick them all off the plant and uncover the
yellow. I have to go back inside and finish cutting my blue fabric."
And off she went, her laughter fading as she closed the front door on
me.

I still say it was a miracle when the yellow pansies bloomed blue.
Maybe it happens only once in a blue moon.

41. Inventory

need new needles," she told me. I was about to open the refrigerator door.

"Do you think they're in the fridge?" I asked.

"No, they're somewhere in my sewing room. Probably in one of the drawers."

"Why do you need new needles?" I asked. She had just recently bought about fifty of them.

"I just broke two seventy-fives," she said.

"You need another size seventy-five then?" I asked.

"No, now I need a ninety."

"And you want me to help you find the needles?" I asked. I suspected that was exactly what she wanted.

"You always find things," she said.

"All right." I followed her down the hall into her sewing room and as she stood aside, I went to her sewing machine and opened up a drawer in the desk next to it. "Here," I said. I pointed to a small package of Schmetz needles.

"They're just more seventy-fives," she said. "I can't find the nineties. I told you that."

"Sorry," I said, and I began searching through the drawers of the desk. I found seven packages of needles.

"They're all for embroidery," she said, her words wiping off the gleeful smile I had on my face at finding them.

"Why don't you have them all in one place?" I said. It was not really a question. I knew she would have no answer. She put things where she put them.

"I was going to, but I got busy," she answered.

"Well, if we find them, how about putting them all in one place."

"All right."

With that promise said aloud, I helped her go through all her drawers, all her bins, all her boxes, all her shelves, all her bags of notions stuck in the corners of the room. We located eighteen packages of needles. Three of the packages were universal size 90 and three were quilting size 90.

"Good, now I can finish quilting," she said as she moved to the sewing machine.

"No," I said.

"No what?" She seemed genuinely puzzled. She had no idea. I took the package of needles and the tool from her hands.

"You're not going to change the needle now. You are not going to make another square or appliqué or anything. You are going to take stock and organize your needles and put them all in one place. Then you are going to do the same with all your quilting notions." I was firm, tough, maybe a bit cruel, but it was for her own good. For mine as well. I had only so many hours in my life to give to searching for lost basting pins or bias tape or rotary cutter blades or templates.

"Now?" she said, bewildered by my request.

"I'll help you," I offered.

"I can't do it now. I have to work on the new quilt."

"Now," I said. You can begin with the needles."

"But…but…."

"Right now," I said. She was frozen in place. I gave her a little nudge. I opened up the first drawer where I had found the embroidery needles. "Start there," I said. "I'll be back in a minute."

I waited until she had actually picked up two packages of the needles, and then I moved quickly out of the room and down the hall toward the garage door.

In the garage I found a small utility box with thirty-six plastic drawers, all large enough for the needles. Of course at that time they each were filled with screws and nails and washers, all carefully sorted years before. I removed the drawers one by one and dumped the hardware from each into a single pile on my workbench. I cleaned the box and took it to her.

She was still standing where I had left her. She still held the two packages of needles. She looked at me. "I don't have anything to put them in," she said as if to explain why she had turned into a statue.

"Here," I said, and I handed her the empty box. "Now put all your needles in the small drawers. Then you can start on the other notions. You can do the thread and the flat head pins and the Celtic bars and the templates and the masking tape."

"That'll take forever," she said.

"That'll take a couple of days, and then you'll be organized and you'll be able to find everything," I said. "Isn't that what you wanted, to be able to find things?"

"I just wanted a new needle," she said.

"Everything else will be a bonus," I said cheerfully. "If you want, I'll help you."

"No, I know how I want everything. I'll do it. But you have to explain to everyone why I'm behind on my quilting."

"I'll tell everyone," I said. And I left her standing there. I was sure that this time, finally, she would do the job.

I didn't see her the rest of the day. At dinner time she came in and ate, quiet the whole time, and then she left the kitchen. "You clean up," she said.

I went to bed while she was still working away. I heard boxes open and close, drawers sliding in and out, little squeals or grunts from her, but I left her alone.

I was awakened in the middle of the night with the bed shaking. The light was on, shining in my sleepy eyes. "What?" I said, wondering what I was doing up.

"I'm done," she said.

"You're all done?" I asked. She had a joyous look on her face.

"Come look," she said.

"Now?" How about morning, late morning?

"Now," she said.

I got up and followed her into the sewing room. I looked. I turned three hundred sixty degrees to see every bit of the room. I looked again. "Nothing's different," I said.

"Wrong," she said. "I took inventory." She pointed to a yellow pad on her desk. I went to it and picked it up.

"What's this?" I asked. She had about fifteen pages full of writing. I looked at her for an explanation.

"I just went through everything and wrote down where everything was. That way I didn't have to move anything. If I want to find something, I just look on the list." She was proud.

"Where are the size ninety quilting needles?" I asked to test her. I watched her face. She frowned then brightened.

"On page three," she said. "Under needles."

I looked. Sure enough, on page three, under needles it listed all her needles and their location. I looked up to see the utility box I had brought her. It was empty.

"I took inventory of everything. It's all there. Now, can I quilt?" she said. She wasn't asking. She had, as usual, passed the test.

I went back to bed, but before I fell asleep I wondered how I was going to sort all the hardware I had dumped and left on my workbench. Maybe I'd just take inventory of it. Washers, screws, nails, etc. Pile Number One. Where was that yellow pad?

42. Fall Break

I have work to do," she said as I stood by the door to her sewing room. She was seated in front of her sewing machine. Her voice came out of her charming mouth, bounced off the chain of triangles she was running through the machine, and careened off the side wall back to me. I guessed that she was working on another quilt.

"You have to get out," I said. She had been working in her room for three days without much of a break except for food and sleep and the necessary but unwelcome trip to the well-euphemized "rest-room." It was the only place she might have rested, but I doubted it.

"I will," she said, adding in a whisper about three seconds later, "eventually."

"It's gorgeous out today and the air is clean and you need to get out of that room," I said, first kindly then more emphatically.

"I have a window. I can see outside," she said. She did have a window, but the shade was down to block out the brilliant sun, and the only light in the room came from the lights over her sewing machine and ironing board. I walked into the room and pulled up the shade.

"Look outside," I said. "You've been locked in this room forever. It's not good for your health. It's probably not good for your quilting." Actually, I don't think any kind of deprivation would interfere with the quality of her quilts.

She lifted her head, cast a quick glance out the window, and went back to her work. "It's nice," she said, but she made no effort to move away from her work.

"I'm turning off the electricity," I said. "You won't be able to quilt," I added dramatically but futilely.

"I can always cut strips of fabric," she said. "And besides, your computer would be off. The refrigerator would be off. Everything you love would be off."

"All right. I give up," I said. But I lied. I moved quickly behind her chair, thrust my hands under her arms, clutched her tightly, and lifted her bodily out of the chair.

She screamed in alarm. "What are you doing?" she asked.

"I'm taking you out of here. You've been inside too long. It's for your own good," I said as I dragged her backwards across the floor. Then I released her long enough to lower my hold on her and lift her up and over my shoulder. I was very glad she weighed less than a pound of feathers.

"Stop it," she said. She was not kicking me or trying to break free. She had her arms thrust out toward the sewing machine, a chain of triangular flags of fabric fluttering, her body trying to get back to where she belonged, but I held her tight in my husbandly grasp. I carried her out of the room, down the hall, and out the front door to the front lawn. There I released her. She held the strip of triangles tightly to her chest.

"OK. I'm outside," she said calmly as she stood free. "It's very nice outside," she said. I relaxed. She would take a deep breath of the air, take in the sight of the leaves begin to turn on the trees running down our block, smell the freshness of the late-blooming flowers around our neighborhood, and then she would be blissful.

Instead, she looked at me, smiled, and turned to run back into the house. A jaguar, the car or the animal, could not have been faster. She was a comic book blur of speed, a contrail of white behind her as she ran back into the house. "I've got quilting to do," she sang in victory as she entered the house and slammed the door behind her. I chased after her, to catch her and bring her back. But I was too slow.

And, of course, the door was locked. But I had a key. I took my time. I knew where to find her. I opened the door and went down the hall to her sewing room. That door, too, was locked. "Honey, let me in," I said.

The door had a lock, but that lock had not been used in nearly twenty years, not since our son used it to lock out his brother for privacy. I banged loudly, desperately, on that locked door.

"Go away," she said.

"Let me in."

"No."

"You need fresh air." I could try logic.

"I just had some."

"Not enough."

"I took a deep breath. It will last me until I've finished my project."

"How long will that be?"

"About three weeks."

"And I won't see you for three weeks?"

"I'll let you see me if you promise not to kidnap me again."

"But you need to get out. You'll waste away in there without sunshine. No vitamin D and your bones will crumble."

"I have my vitamins."

"What kind of vitamins do you have in there?" I asked. Her vitamins were in the kitchen and when she came out to get them, I might have another chance to help her back to sanity.

"Quilting vitamins," she answered.

"What?" I asked. Maybe the door was muffling her words. Maybe my ears were clogged.

"I need my strength to quilt," she said. "Now do you promise to leave me alone until I finish?"

Defeated, I agreed. "All right."

"Good, now why don't you go out for a walk. The fresh air will do you good," she said.

"I think I will," I said, and I did, and it was beautiful out. It still is. And I am waiting. I am still waiting. What kind of quilt takes three weeks?

43. Show Business

She was barking orders to the fabric in her hands, the fabric spread out on the table, the fabric covering her ironing board. "Show me something," she kept saying. "Let's see what you can do," she said over and over. Periodically, she lifted a piece of fabric and brought it up close to her face and stared at it. Then, she held it at arm's length, turned it, reversed it, and put it down flat on the table. Then she took another piece of flowered fabric that had a heart-shaped piece cut out of it. She put that open-hearted piece of fabric over the other and said, "You're good, but you do have a lot of competition," she said. She did this with one piece of fabric after another. After each selection of fabric.

Though I was standing in the doorway leading into her sewing room, I knew she was not talking to me. Though I had often heard her talk to her fabric, I had never heard her talk like that before. She was forceful, assertive, soft and loud and soft again. I watched her a few more minutes before I butted in on her relationship with the fabric. "Is there something new going on here?" I asked.

Whatever she was doing was new to me. I had followed her through every journey into quilting she had made in the past year, and I no longer was surprised by anything she did that might surprise, shock, or bewilder any other person watching her. But though I thought I knew her, her habits, her quirks, her idiosyncrasies, her quilting personalities (and she had several), I had never before seen her behave the way she did yesterday.

"There's no business like show business," she said.

"Ethel Merman," I said, guessing she was testing my memory of the song and who made it famous.

"This isn't a musical," she said. She picked up a piece of marbled yellow fabric. She went through the same procedure as before. She held it close, stared at it, rubbed it between her fingers, looked at it from a distance as she stretched her arm out and then brought it back. She put it flat on the table and put the fabric with the heart-hole over it.

"What are you doing?" I asked straight out. Sometimes it works, sometimes it doesn't.

"Auditions," she said. All right, so frankness and candor and straight talk didn't work.

"Auditions?"

"I'm auditioning the fabric," she said.

"Oh," I said, wondering very much at that moment why I had even entered her room, let alone asked her what I thought was a reasonable question and hoped for a reasonable answer.

"It's not easy to explain," she said.

No, probably not, I thought. Quilting passion never was easy to explain. Madness was more like it. Still, I had been through this before so many times, I thought I would try again. I'd already opened the door, so I might as well go in. But I should have looked where I was going.

"I'll take a difficult explanation," I said bravely.

"It's that new book that came yesterday," she said.

"Another new-book story?" I asked. I should have known. Her quilting book library was getting larger, and so was her ambition to try every new technique she read about.

"*Quilts with a View*," she said.

"Quilts with a philosophy about life?" I asked. Just then I was developing a new philosophy about quilters.

"The author suggests auditioning all the fabric." She was not kidding.

"Have a cattle call?" I knew my show-business terms.

"You have to know what kind of talent the fabric has."

"You're the talent scout?"

"You have to know what kind of potential the fabric has," she said.

"You're the producer?" I went on.

"The winner goes into the view window," she said.

"It's something about a quilt with a view," I said, guessing out loud. I still had no idea.

"It's to choose just the right fabric," she said. "Landscapes need to look correct through the window."

"Is there an award involved with this? A Golden Quilt or something for the winner?"

"The fabric is just happy to be chosen," she said seriously.

"What about the fabric that doesn't make the cut. Don't they deserve something for trying out?" I asked. I could just picture, even if not through a window, all that losing fabric's feelings of rejection.

"I'll audition them again for another quilt," she said.

"That's the way it goes in show business, isn't it," I said, resigned. I saw *Chorus Line* and *Fame*. I know the heartaches and tears. "You dream about success some day, you go to the audition, and you go home a loser," I said.

"The other fabric doesn't lose," she said. "There are no losers in quilting," she said more strongly.

I dried my tears over the fallen cottons. "So, did you choose a winner?" I asked more cheerfully.

"I've narrowed it down to ten," she said.

"A beauty pageant now?"

"They're all beautiful. It's just hard to decide."

"What about a talent contest. Looks aren't everything," I tried.

"Don't you have something else to do?" she asked.

"Probably," I said, thinking about it. "I'll just go sit in the living room and look out the window at the trees out back."

"A tree would look good in a quilt," she said.

"As long as it doesn't have to audition," I said.

44. Lost

I lost her in a quilt shop.

Maybe she lost herself.

How does one get lost in a small shop?

Maybe it wasn't that small.

And when did this happen?

Last Friday.

Early Friday morning.

I drove her to the shop and stopped the car outside the main door. It was eight-fifty-eight and the shop opened at nine.

"Do you have the cash?" I asked her. She patted the pocket in her pants. She wore heavy-duty pants for heavy-duty shopping. She wore a heavy sweatshirt to protect her in the aisles. Shopping for fabric could be dangerous.

"Yes," she answered.

"And you left the checkbook home?"

"Yes," she said.

"And the credit cards?"

"At home," she said.

"No wallet? Nothing hidden away?"

"I set the limit," she said. "I'm not spending a penny more this time."

"Then go for it," I said. She was ready. No matter how much she might lose control, she had limited herself to how much she could spend. In a fabric store, that was wisdom beyond Solomon's. No changing of her mind. No credit card or checkbook available, even if she saw just one more thing she just had to have.

"I'm off," she said.

"I'll pick you up in an hour. Is that enough time?"

"I need only a couple of things. I'll just be looking around after that."

That was the last I heard from her. I watched her go into the shop and I went a few blocks to Wal-Mart to buy some light bulbs.

When I returned an hour later, five minutes late, I expected her to be out on the sidewalk waiting. She wasn't. I turned off the car's engine and went into the shop to get her.

But she wasn't there. She was nowhere in sight. She wasn't at the display of scissors by the cash register. She wasn't at the display of templates by the front door. "My wife," I said to the cashier when he looked at me. He knew Dear Wife and her quilting money quite well.

He nodded. "She's been shopping here," he said with a grin. I supposed my Darling Shopper had spent her limit and the shop had a good day's income already.

"Still looking around, I guess," I said. He nodded. I went to look for her.

The shop was larger than I thought. Though I had been in many times before, I had never gone beyond the front room where large bolts of fabric filled every bit of floor space. The fabric was arranged by colors along one wall. Specialty fabrics were along another. Reproduction fabrics were on two cases down the center of the shop. Batting sat in rolls in bins near the back.

Everything in the shop was arranged in a way guaranteed to invite the fabric maniac to touch and feel and clutch and buy. I know. I had watched my Darling Wife shop in there too often. But she wasn't in that front room, so I moved through an opening between two bolts of muslin and ducked under a Drunkard's Path quilt that hung down too low from the wall above. Two women stood by a revolving stand of quilting books, but my one-and-only wasn't there either.

"Have you seen my Darling Wife?" I asked. The two women looked me up and down, shook their heads, and busied themselves by opening books up and down the rack.

I went on looking. At one point I thought I found her. "Ohhh, this is nice," I heard, but when I went past a cutting table and turned into an alley between bolts of fabrics covered in stars, all I saw was a young teenager swooning at what was probably her first sight of a hundred fat quarters all in one place.

I moved down another row, around another corner, into a room where the walls were hung with miniature quilts. By now I was getting a bit concerned. I was in some labyrinth even a mythical hero could not get out of, and there was no sign of my happy shopper. I started to push aside bolts of fabric, rolls of fabric, boxes of fabric, thinking she might have fainted at the sight of all these riches and fallen into some dark corner. Or she might have been accidentally rolled up into one of the bolts. Well, it might have happened.

I searched and I searched, but to no avail. The back of the small shop became a dark storeroom of dark corridors, the overwhelming smells of musty and dusty fabrics making me gasp and choke. "Honey, where are you?" I bellowed near and far, but no reply came back. Even the chance of an echo was muted by the miles of fabric.

"May I help you?" came a voice then, out of nowhere. I turned around and looked for the source of the voice. No one.

"I'm over here," the voice said, and I turned to see a mystical shape lift up off the floor, and there, from behind a large box of Olfa mats, a small woman emerged. The shop owner. "I was just checking for water damage. We had a small leak in the ceiling," she explained.

"Have you seen my wife?" I asked, never explaining who she was, what she looked like. I assumed the owner would know her. My good wife spent fortunes at this shop.

"She went out back. I told her to wait until they unloaded, but she was eager to see the new shipment."

"Out back. Eager? New shipment?"

The owner laughed. "She couldn't wait to see what was coming in. She went out to the truck to see the new fabric."

"Where?" I asked, and as she pointed into the depths of this tomb of fabrics, I ran toward a small wedge of daylight in the distance. I brushed past stored cartons of books, bolts of fabric, rolls of batting. I pushed my way past sealed boxes of thread and quilting pins and needles. Then I was out into the alley. And there was the truck. And there she was inside the truck. My Darling Wife was rolling a bolt of solid lavender Hoffman Bali to the side of the truck. I watched, shock stopping me in place. She put the bolt next to another one of William Morris black agapanthus. (Don't ask!) Then she turned back and saw me.

"Hi, Hon," she said. "Look what I found."

"I've been looking for you," I said as slowly and calmly as I could. Maybe if I wrapped her in a few bolts of duct tape and kept her at home….

"I'm glad you did. You're just in time. I need some extra money to pay for this fabric. Isn't it nice?"

45. Night Shift

I awoke with a grumble, listened a moment, looked at the clock, and listened again. It was two-fifteen AM, and I heard her fumbling around in the sewing room. I moved to the edge of the bed, leaned out to see into the sewing room, and saw the small light was on over her sewing machine. Now what?

It wasn't that she was an insomniac. No, she just woke up a lot during the night. Usually she went back to sleep. But she was not sleeping now. If I was correct, and I had the experience to know, she would soon be quilting. She had become a nocturnal quilter, though I always worried that she would be quilting in her sleep and sew herself up in about ten yards of fabric.

As I had to be up anyway in three or four hours, I got out of bed and stumbled sleepily into the sewing room. "What are you doing?" I asked.

"Oh, you're up already?" she asked.

"The earthquake woke me," I said. I leaned against the doorjamb.

"There wasn't any earthquake," she said. "Was there?"

"You turned on your sewing machine," I said.

"And that woke you up?"

"I was getting up anyway. So what are you doing?"

"I'm going to finish the foot quilt."

"You're doing that now?"

"Well, I was up, so it seemed the right thing to do."

"You having trouble sleeping again?"

"No, I'm always up this time of morning. You know that."

"But you usually go back to sleep."

"Your quilt cried out to be finished."

"That's probably what woke me up," I said. "You know how I can't sleep when there's crying going on."

"It wasn't crying, not like with tears. It kind of shouted, quietly."

The quilt shouted quietly? "Well, it woke me up," I said. I swayed from one side of the doorway to the other.

"Go back to bed," she said.

"I can't. I'm up now."

"Do you have insomnia?" she asked.

"No, I don't have insomnia. I have trouble sleeping when your projects cry out in the night and the switch on your sewing machine screams out for me to wake up."

"I should have closed the door."

"Maybe." I yawned and slid down the jamb to the floor.

"I'm just going to finish this and then go back to sleep," she said.

"Zzzzzzzzzz."

"Wake up a minute," I heard her say somewhere in the distance.

"Umm, what?" I asked. For some reason I was on the floor.

"I want you to try this," she said. I peeked out under heavy eyelids. She held up a very small quilt.

"Now?"

"I want you to be happy with it," she said. She was coming over to me. She helped me up.

"You mean you want my feet to be happy," I said, yawning again. The small quilt was to cover a part of the large quilt on our bed. She didn't want me to put my feet up on the bed and ruin the quilt when sometimes I lay there to read during the day or look out the window at the trees and birds. I tried to remember to spread out a towel for my shoes, but sometimes I forgot. So, when she complained, I suggested she make a quilt for my feet. She grumbled and said I was foolish, that there was no such thing as a foot quilt, that she didn't have time or fabric to waste on my feet when I could just take my shoes off now and then.

"It takes time to take off my shoes and put them back on," I had said. "It takes more time to take my shoes off than to lie down." In a moment of brilliance, I also told her that she could invent a foot quilt if not having heard of one or seen one before was what was bothering her. Now, apparently, she had done just that.

"Just try this out," she said sweetly.

She pushed me into the bedroom and forced me down on the bed. My legs were stretched out and she lifted my bare feet to settle down on the new foot quilt. "This is all done, then?" I asked.

"I finished it. You've been asleep half an hour."

"I have?" Was it just possible that I had fallen asleep in the doorway of her sewing room?

"It works fine, doesn't it?" She pointed at my feet. I looked at my feet.

Beneath my amazed feet was a patchwork fantasy of fabric she had sewn together into a colored frenzy of a quilt. She hadn't wasted any expensive, high quality, or even good fabric. It seemed as if she had emptied her scrap basket onto her sewing machine and miraculously bound the scraps together into a two-foot-square foot quilt. It was no quilt design anyone had ever seen before, but to me and my feet it was beautiful.

"Of course it works fine," I agreed. My feet were in love with the quilt. "Can I go back to sleep now?" I pleaded.

"If you want to sleep your life away," she said.

"Not my whole life. Just a few hours." I closed my eyes.

"What about a quilt for the hassock in the living room?"

"What about it?" I opened my eyes. I looked at her.

"Didn't you want me to make a quilt for your feet there, too?"

"Now?"

"Now is a good time," she said.

And now it was…for her. She went off back to her sewing room, but I stayed where I was and closed my eyes again. I lay there on top of the bed with my feet happily stretched out on the foot quilt. And, I know, I slept just fine.

46. Unmistake

*T*here really shouldn't be any un's in quilting," she said to me yesterday morning, and I didn't blink. I waited for her to go on, for there had to be a message in her words. If I waited long enough, I would be able to decode her cryptic words.

But she didn't go on. She brewed some herbal tea and took her yogurt out of the refrigerator.

"So?" I finally asked.

"So, I have to unsew today, and I don't want to unsew."

"Certainly not," I said. I knew I, myself, would never unsew, whatever technique of quilting that turned out to be. I have spent about ninety-nine percent of my time the last year learning to understand her, but it has been an endless task. Just when I thought I had heard everything one small quilting lady had to say, she surprised me with something new. All I could do was I make some room in the remnants of my brain and wait for a response to see if I could fit it in.

"If I didn't make mistakes—," she began.

"Oh, no, not again!" Once she began mourning and wailing about the lost stitch, the wrong color, the crooked bias, the wrong weight batting, the accidental scrap of polyester mixed with the cotton, the slanted seam, the four-cornered triangle, or whatever other imperceptible flaw she saw in her quilting, then I knew I had to pay attention and be ready to offer enough support to get her back to normal.

"Do you want to see it?" she asked.

"Do I have a choice?" I replied out of her hearing.

"Wait here," she said. She put her yogurt down on the table and disappeared from the room. I sipped my coffee and did some relaxation exercises. I needed to be calm during the next few minutes.

She returned with her latest project in hand. She held out a small, small miniature quilt top she had been working on. It was a paper-pieced butterfly. It was about nine inches by eleven. I knew that because she had told me before she had started it that she was going to quilt a nine-by-eleven-inch paper-pieced quilt. I listened. I remembered. If I hadn't, if I had paid her no heed when she explained her quilting to me, she would have long before used me for trapunto, stuffing me into one of her quilts piece by piece. (Actually, she hasn't done any trapunto yet, but just in case.)

"Do you see it?" she asked. It was a test. Somewhere in that letter-sized paper-pieced butterfly design in the teeny quilt she was holding was a flaw. I had to find it or fail one of life's major tests.

I looked. I examined. I peered. I inspected. Finally, I took a chance. "The bottom of the butterfly," I said.

"Yes!" she said. It was the bong for a correct answer.

"It's just a little off," I said. One tiny piece the size of an emaciated ant met another piece one one-thousandth of an inch off.

"So you know why I have to unsew it?" she asked. She was asking if I knew why rain fell down instead of up.

"Unsew?" I asked. It was still a strange word. I knew about ripping, and I knew about throwing away and starting over. I knew about cutting out, and I knew about putting away in a drawer for ten years. I even knew about resewing. She was right about too many un's.

"It's paper-piecing, and it's impossible to fix. So I'm going to try to unsew it until I get to the mistake and then sew it the right way."

"You can do that?" I asked.

"No, I don't think so," she said, surprising me.

"You mean you can't rip out the stitches and fix it?"

"I have to unsew it," she insisted.

"But you don't think you can do that?"

"I know I can't. I need to take a class in unsewing."

"I never heard of a class in unsewing."

"They should have one somewhere."

"And until they do?" She was troubled, perplexed, and pessimistic.

"I'll have to think of something else," she said. She lowered her head and looked miserable.

"It's only a very small, small, little, tiny mistake in a very small, small quilt."

"Small is difficult to do," she said.

"Sometimes it is," I agreed. I was helpless to help her. "But you can do it, you know."

"I'll try," she said.

That was yesterday. This morning she shook me awake, a shaking I had long before learned to live with when she took up quilting as her life's work. "It's all right now," she said, dangling the handkerchief-sized quilt in front of my half-open (or half-closed) eyes.

"You unsewed it?" I yawned at her.

"No."

I opened my eyes fully, reached for my glasses on the headboard, put them on, and looked at the butterfly unfluttering in her hand. "No?" I asked.

"Can you tell what I did?" she asked.

"You made it better," I guessed.

"How did I make it better?" she asked. I looked carefully at the butterfly, stared at the place that had been, in her eyes, a blemish, a disfigurement, an atrocity of no mean proportions. I saw a happy butterfly standing proud.

"Tell me how," I said.

"I emended it," she said.

"You emended it?"

She didn't answer. She smiled and took herself and her untainted, unblotched, unbungled quilt top away. I lay there in bed thinking about quilters and how they worked in mysterious ways.

47. The Mule

She was standing in the middle of her sewing room. She swayed slightly from front to back and then side to side. Her face had a look of total puzzlement on it, her eyes dull, her cheeks slightly flushed. I watched her a moment. Though I had seen her in a dozen odd poses since she had begun quilting, I had never seen her quite like this. I was soon puzzled myself.

"Are you all right?" I finally asked.

"I'm fine," she said.

"What are you doing?" Watching her gave me no clue.

"Trying to decide," she said. She spoke with a sigh between each breath.

"What are you trying to decide?" I asked. The conversation seemed to be going very slowly, her lips hiding her words like some ventriloquist's.

"I can't decide what to quilt next," she said. She looked straight at me, but her look seemed empty. The normal sparkle was gone from her eyes.

Now, this was a very strange event going on. I thought of calling the newspaper to send a reporter to take it down. I even thought of CNN or MSNBC. The fact that she was hesitating for even a moment over what to quilt next was equal to any top news event. "Just pick something. Anything," I said.

"I can't," she said, resignation in her voice, gloom in her voice. I did not know this woman.

"You'll starve to death," I said.

"What? I'm not hungry." Her face changed that moment from a look of dismay to a look of wonder at what crazy statement her husband had come up with.

"Remember the mule," I said.

"What mule? I'm not quilting a mule. Do you see a mule in here?" Now she was a bit more animated.

"The mule that stood midway between two stacks of hay and couldn't decide which one to eat. It finally starved to death from indecision."

"I'm not a mule. I can decide."

"All right, decide." I went to her sewing table where she had laid out several books open to quilting projects, several samples of fabric laid out as well. "Pick one," I said pointing to one quilt pattern after another. "Go ahead," I dared her.

Her eyes moved back and forth, she licked her upper lip, she swiveled her head, she bobbed her head, and then she shook it. Finally she sighed a long sigh. "I can't." On her forehead, beads of sweat danced like drops of water on a hot iron. Her own iron, needless to say, sat cold on the ironing board.

"Do this one," I said, grabbing a book of patterns for miniature quilts. "Why don't you make this flower garden?" I asked.

"I'm not sure," she said doubtfully.

"All right," I said, "I'll go get one of the spinners from the grandkids' game box and we'll label all the different types of quilts and you can spin for a winner."

"My head is already spinning," she said, and she did have a dizzy look now.

"We'll roll dice," I suggested.

"No, there aren't enough combinations."

"How many projects do you have?" I asked. Another in a long list of imbecilic questions.

"I'm up to twenty-seven. That's what caused the problem. I started opening the quilt books, and I liked this quilt and that quilt and I want to do them all, but I can't decide."

"How about a game of Pin the Tail on a Project?" I said. I'll blindfold you and spin you around three times. You do have a pin in here somewhere?"

"How about I stick a pin in you?" she said, "You're not helping me decide."

"Do you want me to pick one?" Uh-oh, I knew what would happen. If I picked one, she would ask me what was wrong with the other twenty-six.

"No. It's my responsibility. Just give me some more time."

"How much time?"

"Two weeks?" she asked.

"Is that a question?"

"I don't know how long. What should I do?"

"Ask me," I said.

"Ask you?" Now she seemed more bewildered than before.

"If I decide, then you're off the hook," I said graciously.

"Do you think…?"

"Ask me," I said. How difficult was it to pick a quilt? All the choices were fine with me.

Well, she thought about that, and while she did, I thought about that as well. I realized I had no idea what kind of quilt she would want to make next. And if I suggested one and she didn't like my choice, then what?

"All right," she said. "What do you think?" She looked at me with hope.

"I think you should decide," I said. I wanted to be alive and well when this crisis was over.

That was yesterday. Today, as I was trying to decide what to have for lunch, a tuna salad or a chicken sandwich, a bowl of soup or a bowl of stew, a burrito or a taco, I heard her open the front door.

"Going somewhere?" I asked.

"I need to get some new fabric," she said as she ran from the house toward the front walk. The door was swinging closed behind her.

"New fabric?" I called out between the door and the doorjamb. She had enough fabric in the house to make a quilt large enough to cover the earth.

"For my new project," she said from farther down the walk. The door was almost closed.

"You decided what project you're going to do next?" I yelled after her.

"I decided I need new fabric before I can decide," she said, and with that the door slammed shut. I went back to the kitchen. I decided on tuna. I was no mule.

PART 12

48. A "Real" Man

There's an article in one of my quilting magazines where someone says men shouldn't be allowed in quilt shops," Darling Wife said. She looked at me for a response.

"Hah!" I replied.

That was two months ago. Today she came to me with the new issue and letters from readers responding to the article about men in quilt shops and fabric stores. "There's a fight going on," she said.

"What's the fight about?" I asked. It seemed many fights broke out in the world of quilting. We tried to stay away from them, but this was a global village we now lived in, this earth of ours, and sometimes we couldn't avoid the battle. In this case, the arguments were about people called, well, "men."

"Some of the women say they won't allow their husbands to go with them, and some argue that their husbands don't want to go, but a few stick up for their husbands; they say having them go along is a blessing."

"And which side are you on?" I knew how she would answer. She believes I go with her because I enjoy finding things for her to buy. Now, why does she have that idea?

"I'm on your side, whatever it is," she said diplomatically.

"What do the men say?"

"One man says he'd rather have root-canal work in each and every one of his teeth than go inside a quilt shop."

"Sounds as if he doesn't want to go along," I said wisely.

"Another man wrote that he likes to go because then he can stand around outside the shop with the other men and talk about sports and politics."

"A lot of men do that," I said. "There aren't that many places anymore where men can gather." I had joined such a group once when I was new to my wife's passion for quilting and shopping for fabric. The men that day stood around outside the quilt shop and talked about how much money their wives were spending. They even took bets as to how long the shopping would take. I left the group early and went inside. I wanted to tell all the women to stay for several hours.

"Of course, there are reasons why the men don't go in," my wife began. "Some of the men say that when they go inside, the women frown at them for being there and the clerks neglect them and then they feel out of place. They'd rather stay home than get that kind of treatment."

"Considering how few men we see, most of them do stay home."

"Do you ever get that feeling about being not wanted? Some of the men feel that."

"I've never felt that," I said. I never had. Oh, I may have had a strange look now and then, or a woman might have tried to grab some fat quarter out of my hand, and I did have one woman yell at me when I got to a quilt book before she did, but all in all, I and the other men inside that I talked to were generally welcome. It's true that there weren't many.

"Someone wrote that her husband works on his truck outside the store while she's inside. One day she got to buy out the whole store because each time she was finished and came out, he had more of his truck apart."

"I can believe that. I once saw a man jog around the parking lot while he waited. He was wearing an exercise outfit and had on running shoes. Each time he made a lap he looked in through the window to see if his wife was done yet. He must have lost thirty pounds by the time she came out."

"And what were you doing at that time? You're never outside waiting."

"I was getting the batting for you, and the shelves were right next to the window."

"Well, here's a woman who wrote that her husband got so embarrassed by all those women in one place that he turned red and the color stuck to him, just frozen in place. His wife wants him to go to work as a stop sign."

"Now you're making that up," I said. Though it was possible. I have seen men blush as they accompanied their wives through the store. One man once went faint when a woman grabbed at his shirt, moved herself right up next to him, rubbed her hand across his chest, and told him the design on his shirt would make a great quilt design.

"So what do you think can be done about it?" she asked, suddenly serious.

"Done about what?"

"All these men who can't or won't go into a quilt shop with their wives," she answered.

"I'd have all the quilt shops put in a coffee bar where the men can sit, drink coffee, and talk about what it's like to be married to a woman who quilts."

"That might work. I could use a cup of coffee once in a while. I don't know how other women would feel."

"How many wives do you think want their husbands along?" I asked.

"I don't know. A few maybe."

"And how long do you think it will be before men invade the quilt shops?"

"Probably years."

"Then forget it. There's not much we can do," I said.

"We can go shopping, and you can write and tell everyone what it's like to be a real man."

"To be a 'real' man when it comes to shopping in a quilt store?" I asked. The other ways were private.

"You can be a role model. Just your being seen inside can set an example in every fabric store or quilt shop in town. Then we can go from town to town. You could start a new men's movement."

I wondered if, just maybe, I really was needed out there. A men's quilting movement for the twenty-first century? A Million-Man March into quilt shops? It might just work. "And what'll you do to help?" I asked.

"I'll shop more."

Of course.

49. Inspired

I'm giddy," she said.

"What?" I said.

"My brain is floating."

"Are you dizzy?" I asked, concerned. We were in Denver, Pennsylvania, in Sauder's Fabrics, the first of fifteen shops and homes we were to visit the next three days. It was our first morning driving the country roads around Lancaster in her quest to see five million quilts. We had just entered into a world of quilt fabrics, fabrics she had promised on the plane she would only look at and never buy. Hah!

"I feel wonderful," she said as her words trailed behind her. She was Alice in the wonderland of fabric, bolts and bolts of fabric.

I caught up with her. "So is your head all right now?" I asked as she wrapped her arms around a bolt of fabric. I wasn't really sure.

"I'm in love," she said.

"I hope so," I replied. We were soon coming up on our thirty-ninth anniversary. I hoped she was referring to me.

""I'm so giddy," she said again as she unfurled a yard of green fabric. "Grass," she said.

I looked around for a phone. I wondered if ambulances came this far out into the Pennsylvania countryside. "Where does it hurt?" I said as I prepared to catch her if she fainted.

"This is perfect for the grass on the quilt I want to make," she said.

I looked at the fabric she was caressing. It did, indeed, look like grass. "Then you're not ill?" I asked just to be sure.

"It's Eden," she said.

"What?" She handed me the bolt of green.

"Three yards," she said, pointing me toward the cutting table at the front of the shop.

"But, you said…." She didn't hear me. She squealed as she went toward another bolt. This one was sky blue.

"All the fabric I've been looking for," she said.

Now, I was puzzled. We had visited dozen and dozens of quilt shops in the past year, and we both had decided she had seen every fabric known. Adding her access to the Internet's quilt sites, I believed she had seen it all. Wrong.

"Now I understand," she said as she moved down the aisle touching bolt after bolt, her eyes ablaze, glazed. "I'm in Candy Land," she said. "I've heard people talk about the euphoric feeling they get when they walk into a room of fabric like this," she explained.

Now this is one woman who does not normally allow her emotions to overwhelm her. But here she was, babbling in a warehouse-sized room of fabric just yards from a field where sheep grazed. She handed me another bolt of fabric, just the brick pattern she needed for a house appliqué.

"Three yards," she said.

And so it went. And went. And went. "Giddy" wasn't a strong enough word for the lightness of her head. She was floating above the atmosphere, oxygen deprived. I ran back and forth to the counter to have the fabric cut, each piece piled on another. Then, as I faced exhaustion, she was done. "I'm done here," she said.

That was the beginning. By the end of the first day we had visited three Amish homes and four quilt shops. The rented car would likely be stopped for inspection the way it bulged.

The next day it continued. We visited the People's Place Quilt Museum in the town of Intercourse. "I feel giddy, oh so giddy," she sang as she wandered among Amish and Mennonite quilts. She stopped. She stared. She sighed. She went on. "I'm going to need more fabric," she said.

"We'll have to pay for the extra weight on the plane," I said, hoping to dissuade her.

"It's all so inspiring," she said.

"I'm perspiring," I said, as I realized we still had two days to go.

"I'm going Amish," she said.

"You already did Amish," I said. She had already made me a lovely queen-sized Amish-style quilt.

"Do you see these?" she chided. "There are a lot of different types of quilts here," she said.

"That's a lot of quilting to do," I said. I had to get her back to reality.

"I'll make small ones. Paper-pieced Amish-style quilts. Lots and lots of them," she said.

"And what about all the fabric you bought for the other quilts you plan to make?"

"They can wait. Amish first. All solids. Mennonite quilts have prints in them." She was looking at the brochure she had picked up at the entrance to the museum.

"Can we go now?" I asked. It had been two hours and three trips around the museum. I was getting hungry again. I just wondered if we would have money for food after moving downstairs to the fabric section.

"I want to stop in the fabric section downstairs," she said.

"After lunch," I said.

We ate in a small lunchroom down the street. Afterward, as we were walking down the street, I turned to her to comment on the number of Amish people in the restaurant, but she was not walking next to me. I turned and saw her entering another quilt shop, the next one on our list. I ran after her. Too late. She had found another Paradise.

I found her looking at John Deere fabric. "We don't live on a farm," I said.

"I'm just looking," she said. "I don't have to buy everything," she said.

"No, of course you don't." But she had to buy almost everything.

"I feel…," she began.

"Giddy," I finished.

"So inspired," she corrected.

"Fabric inspires you. Quilts inspire you. The sky and the sun and the moon inspire you. When it comes to quilts, mud and garbage and mold and manure inspire you, too," I said.

"When we get home, I'm going to show you," she said. If we ever got home.

On the way home, the pilot of the plane said we were encountering turbulence as the plane bumped along its flight pattern now and then, but I knew it wasn't air currents that caused everyone to stay strapped in by their seat belts. It was the extra weight the plane carried. It was fabric. It was my wife's head, heavy with inspiration. As for me, I was just giddy to be going home.

50. Invasion

It was an invasion. No doubt. There were signs everywhere. The last vestige of my freedom was in jeopardy. I had to defend myself with all the might I had. And most of all, she had made no effort to hide her tracks. The evidence was overwhelming. Confrontation was the only way. I had to defend my way of life.

"You don't have enough room in the rest of the house?" I asked before she had a chance to deny anything.

"What?" she replied.

"Don't play the innocent with me," I said.

"What are you talking about?"

"Your sewing room and quilting room and cutting room are not big enough?"

"My rooms?" She looked bewildered, but I had seen that put-on look before. She was a master of disguise. Once she had become a quilter, I could expect anything from her.

"I still remember when you took over the pantry," I said. It wasn't long into her quilting that I went to find some canned peaches. But instead of the shelf full of fruit I expected, I found that she had taken over yet another room, and she had left little enough space for the food we had stored away. If there were a blizzard or a flood or a hurricane or an earthquake, what could a cutting table and six shelves full of fabric do to feed us?

"That was a long time ago," she said. "What are you hinting at?"

"I'm not hinting. I found you out. Quilting creep won't work this time."

She looked at me with those virtuous eyes. "Quilting creep?"

"You know what I mean," I accused. "First, just a corner of the back room for your quilting supplies. Then another corner for a second sewing machine. Then the middle of the room for your ironing board. Then all the bookshelves for your stash. Then the old stereo cabinet for your templates and rulers and squares. And you have a closet full of quilting thread. I should have known from the beginning that the quilt creep wouldn't end. First an inch, then a mile," I said knowingly. I pointed my finger at her. "You already have most of the house. Now you want more." I pointed all my ten fingers at her. She pulled herself back away from me. She knew she was guilty.

"Quilting takes a lot of space. You have a computer room."

"Aha!" I said. She knew what I was saying. "So you admit to quilting creep?"

"I don't admit to anything I don't understand. If you're talking about crepe…."

"Don't confuse the issue with fabric—or a silly French pancake. I'm talking about how you took over the bookshelves when you ran out of room. I'm talking about how you took over the cupboards in the kitchen. I'm talking about how the hall closets contain your exploding volume of stash. I'm talking about your sneaking around to take over the computer room now." She looked at me, her eyes, her face, and her body all trying to convey innocence. "Maybe you're right," I continued. I was not fooled by her duplicity. "It's not just creep. It's not crawl. It's an all-out invasion."

"I don't want your computer room," she said as she turned away.

"Oh, no?" I moved to face her again. "Then why is my desk in there covered with your paper? Paper squares and paper triangles everywhere." I had her. She squirmed. She was wrapped in guilt. I had the evidence and I was confronting her and she knew she was trapped.

"Did I leave something in there?" she asked, feigning ignorance again.

"All over the place. It must be winter because there's a blizzard of paper in there."

"I was just using the copy machine to copy some paper-piecing patterns."

"Aha! You admit it!"

"I admit I'm making a wall-hanging."

"Another wallhanging? You want my walls too, don't you." I had seen the walls of the house disappear one by one, surrendering themselves to wallhangings and little quilts and big quilts. Soon she'd need swing-out quilt racks on every wall, and she would give out white gloves to every visitor, as she displayed her work on the swinging racks, one after another.

"You have all the walls in your computer room covered with photos and posters and computer stuff, don't you?"

"I admit that. Those are the only walls I have left. Do you admit trying to take over the whole house?"

"Yes."

"You do?" This was too easy. She should have fought more. I expected her to shout her defiance.

"Yes," she said, "and do you know those two empty drawers and that shelf in your desk?" She smiled a treacherous smile. She grinned. She gloated. There was evil in her smile.

Gulp! "Yes?"

"They're not empty anymore. Neither is the top shelf above the computer or the space under the desk." She was breathing more heavily. "I want it all and I am taking it all. This will soon be a total quilting house." Her eyes were glazed over, her face flushed with power. I expected to see foam coming out of her mouth next.

"You can't have my side of the bed," I said, defiantly. It could soon be all I had left. I would fight to the end.

"I don't need your side of the bed," she replied quietly. Her face became soft and she smiled sweetly now. "Not yet."

51. Think Quilts

"The walls need quilts," she said.

"What?" I asked. I didn't think before asking the question. It was an automatic response to certain types of sounds that came out of her mouth, those that related in some way to her quilting.

"They're so bare," she said. "Don't you think so?"

"I think your mind is bare," I said. Lately, I had been thinking up dozens of new responses to use on her when she made some reference to the life she had left behind for a month. It was at her request.

Four weeks before, she had said that on our trip to England she would need all the help she could get to keep her mind off quilting at home. Though we visited seven quilt shops and bought several "foreign" quilt magazines published in Britain and Australia, she had been faithful to her promise to enjoy the trip and not think about all the quilting she had waiting. But as the weeks went on, her pledge of abstinence became more difficult to uphold. More and more she was thinking quilts. Five days before we were to come home, she began to crack.

"War is hell," she said.

"Yes," I agreed, thinking about NATO and Serbia and Kosovo as we walked in tunnels dug deep into the White Cliffs of Dover where the British command was set up during the Second World War. We were at Dover Castle in Dover, England, on a tour of the underground tunnels where brave people had spent years defending freedom.

"It would have been better if there had been quilts on the tunnel walls," she said.

"You're probably right," I said, thinking of the horror of the bombing made lighter by a bucolic farm scene quilt hanging from the chalk walls.

A day later her absence from quilting got her going again. "They need quilts down here," she said.

"What?" We were in one of the deep underground tube stations below Picadilly Circus, waiting to board the next train that came along.

"All these underground tube tunnels," she said, "they should have some nice quilts on the walls instead of all those travel posters."

"Quilts in the stations?" I asked, knowing full well what she was suggesting.

"Why not? Every time people go underground they could see Amish quilts and watercolor quilts and Stack-n-Whack quilts and paper-pieced flowered quilts, and even Sunbonnet Sue quilts. These walls would be great for hanging quilts."

"Good idea," I said as a train roared into the station.

She said the same in Paddington Station, where we waited for an early-morning train to take us to the English countryside.

"Up there," she said as she pointed up at the huge board that listed the train schedules and the platforms the trains would depart from.

"Up there, what?" I asked as I looked for our train.

"Quilts," she said.

"I don't see any quilts," I said.

"Not yet, but if they put quilts up there, all the people waiting would have something to look at until their train information was posted."

"That's true," I agreed, as I looked at the hundreds of people with their heads craned toward the signs above. I looked up and imagined a row of giant quilts, but then I got a stiff neck.

"Quilts in every window of Harrods," she said as we passed by one of the world's most famous department stores. "Everyone knows what a department store sells inside," she hurried on. "Instead of all that furniture and the clothes and the exotic gifts, there can be a nice quilt in each window. Thousands of people pass by here every day. They could look at quilts from all over Great Britain and the rest of the world."

"I'll put that idea in the suggestion box," I said as I hurried her by the store before she wanted to go in and find out that the famous food halls needed quilts in the bakery or meat market or tea shop.

"Do you think someone could make a really big quilt?" she said.

"What?"

"Maybe a guild or several guilds working together," she said.

I looked around for a wall or a fence she might have just chosen for another quilt site there in London. All I saw was the Parliament Building and the tower that held Big Ben. "Oh, no," I said.

"Oh, no, what?" she asked.

"No one wants to hang a quilt up there," I said.

"Not there," she said. "Don't be silly. I was thinking about the fence around Westminster Abbey."

"You want to hang quilts around Westminster Abbey?" Why not? She would make a quilt to hang from London Bridge if she had the chance.

"It's an idea," she said.

I had been wrong to think that spending a month away from her quilting, away from her stash and sewing machine, away from her books and supplies, away from her Internet quilt lists, would turn her into an ordinary tourist. Nothing about a quilter is ordinary. Even though she had pledged, promised, affirmed, and even sworn on a copy of her favorite quilt magazine that she would not think about quilting while we were in London, she had succumbed, given in, surrendered. Her blood, made up mostly of fabric and thread, was thicker than any promises.

Now that we are back home and she is busy finishing up a quilt she had begun before we left, she hasn't said a word about decorating England with quilts. But just because she hasn't mentioned it doesn't mean she hasn't been thinking about it. This morning I saw her look at the photos we had taken on our trip, and every once in a while she looked at one a long time and sighed. After the seventh sigh, I asked her, "What are you thinking?"

"Oh, nothing much. I was just remembering when we went to Greenwich and stood on the time line where the sign said the millennium began."

"And?"

"Maybe I should make a millennium quilt and send it to them...."

52. Counter Measure

Coffee! I needed coffee. I rolled off the edge of the bed, crawled on my knees until I got a grip on the headboard, and lifted myself unsteadily until I was standing. My body listed from side to side as I went down the hall. Finally, my head dull and my body still asleep, I reached the kitchen. I pushed myself along the counter until I reached the coffeemaker. I reached for the handle of the carafe and the handle was missing. The whole carafe was missing. The coffeemaker was missing.

"The coffeemaker's missing," I said to my Darling Wife, who had gone to the kitchen long before me. But, there was no answer. She was missing as well. I looked again for the coffeemaker. The spot where it sat faithfully every morning was empty. The area around the coffeemaker was empty too. I reached for the toaster oven, but it was gone. The breadmaker was gone. The knife block was missing. "Everything's missing," I said to my missing wife. The whole counter was empty. Every appliance we owned and loved and that kept us alive and well each day was missing. "Help," I said as I began to collapse back into sleep. "Burglars," I said as I sat down heavily at the kitchen table.

"What burglars?" I heard as my head dipped toward the table top. It was the voice of salvation coming through the doorway from the garage off the kitchen.

"The coffeemaker's gone. Everything's gone," I said.

"I'm cleaning the counter," she said as she stepped into the room. She had a can of Ajax in one hand and a bottle of 409 in the other.

"You're cleaning the counter?" I asked, unsure that I was speaking to the love of my life. Why was she cleaning the counter at four in the morning? "Why are you cleaning the counter before breakfast?" I asked, though I knew it was foolish to ask.

"It's the only place long enough to baste the quilt," she said as she put down the can and the bottle and picked up a sponge and began wiping at the counter top. "I measured it."

"You measured the counter?"

"Of course," she said.

Now, a man in better condition, a man who had already had his coffee and was alert to the world, a man who had lived with this quilting lady and understood every quirk, every idiosyncrasy a quilter might have, that man might have understood. But just then I was not that man. So I had to ask. "Why?"

"The table runner quilt won't fit on the kitchen table," she said as she rubbed at black spots left by the rubber feet of the heavy breadmaker.

"You made a table runner that was too big for the table and it's now a counter runner?" I asked. It sounded like a good question to my brain, though my brain felt as though it had a breadmaker in it.

"It's just too big for our table. It's not too big for every table," she said. She began wiping the counter clean with a wet dishcloth.

The toaster joined the breadmaker in my head. "What?"

"I need to baste the table runner I'm making for your brother. He has a big table. We have a small table. I knew you wouldn't want me to wake you up to drag out the banquet tables and set them up, so I looked around for a place to baste the quilt top to the batting and the backing and there's no other place in the house."

"No, there's no other place," I agreed. I knew why there was no other place in our house. She had taken it all. Slowly, openly, and without a qualm, like an oil slick spreading over the ocean from an oil spill from a tanker, she and her quilting had taken over every inch of the house. Her fabric stashes (yes, plural), her batting, her sewing machines, her storage bins, her notions, her quilt books, all had joined in a conspiracy to cover the world. But the kitchen counter?

"Where's the coffee maker?" I asked.

"On the cutting table," she said. She dried the counter top.

"Is it all right to make coffee in there?" I asked, moving toward the cutting room just off the other side of the kitchen.

"Of course," she said.

"Thank you," I said.

That was, of course, in the early morning. By mid-morning she had her quilt sandwich spread out over the counter, a counter that previously had known only about turkey sandwiches and peanut butter and jelly sandwiches and toast and coffee and bread. I watched her begin to put in the small brass-coated number-one safety pins one by one. She turned and saw me watching her.

"It's just the right height," she said. "It's so comfortable to work at this level." She smiled. It was a quilter's smile, the worst kind.

"No," I said, understanding that smile too well. She was planning to capture and occupy the last free space left in the house, perhaps for all time. Where was NATO when I needed it?

"My back doesn't hurt working here," she said. She had a dozen pins in, all of them still open. She would take her little wooden Kwik Klip and close them all after they were all in. I had once tried helping her close the pins and had lost twelve fingers or so in the attempt.

"It's a counter top," I said quickly. "It's for toasters and coffee makers and teapots and breadmakers," I added in panic. I couldn't let her have it.

"Just once in a while," she said, that impish smile still spread across her devious face.

"How often is that?" I asked. Once, a long time ago in a land far away, she had told me she was only going to quilt once in a while. Hah!

"The counter's only wide enough for a table runner," she said, "a long table runner that won't fit anywhere else."

"You promise?" I asked. What is a quilter's promise worth? Do quilters know right from wrong? Are they even aware of their surroundings?

"For now," she said.

I just had a cup of coffee. I made it at the counter. The table runner is basted and back in the sewing room ready to be quilted. The coffee maker and all the other appliances are back now where they belong. All's right with the kitchen. For now.

Order Form

Additional copies of

52 Weeks of Quilting

are available from:

A.B. Silver
P.O. Box 130641
Carlsbad, CA 92013

$15.95 plus shipping ($3.50 first book/$1 for each additional book)
(California residents add $1.32 state tax per book.)

Please send name, address, and phone (in case your order goes astray).
If the book is a gift, we will include a gift card from you.

Also available in *A Year in the Life* series:

12 Months of Sewing

Same price, same order address, same offer of a gift card.

Stories by Popser